Direct Cost and Contribution Accounting

WILEY SERIES ON SYSTEMS AND CONTROLS FOR FINANCIAL MANAGEMENT

Edited by Robert L. Shultis and Frank M. Mastromano

Direct Cost and Contribution Accounting

AN INTEGRATED MANAGEMENT ACCOUNTING SYSTEM

GERMAIN BÖER

Associate Professor of Accounting
College of Business Administration
Oklahoma State University

A WILEY-INTERSCIENCE PUBLICATION

JOHN WILEY & SONS, New York • London • Sydney • Toronto

Copyright © 1974, by John Wiley & Sons, Inc.

All rights reserved. Published simultaneously in Canada.

No part of this book may be reproduced by any means, nor
transmitted, nor translated into a machine language without the written permission of the publisher.

Library of Congress Cataloging in Publication Data:

Böer, Germain, 1937–
  Direct cost and contribution accounting.

  (Wiley series on systems and controls for
financial management)
  "A Wiley-Interscience publication"
  Includes bibliographies.
  1. Cost accounting. I. Title.

HF5686.C8B593   657'.42   73-17324
ISBN 0-471-08505-7

Printed in the United States of America

10 9 8 7 6 5 4 3 2

SERIES PREFACE

No one needs to tell the reader that the world is changing. He sees it all too clearly. The immutable, the constant, the unchanging of a decade or two ago no longer represent the latest thinking—on *any* subject, whether morals, medicine, politics, economics, or religion. Change has always been with us, but the pace has been accelerating, especially in the postwar years.

Business, particularly with the advent of the electronic computer some 20 years ago, has also undergone change. New disciplines have sprung up. New professions are born. New skills are in demand. And the need is ever greater to blend the new skills with those of the older professions to meet the demands of modern business.

The accounting and financial functions certainly are no exception. The constancy of change is as pervasive in these fields as it is in any other. Industry is moving toward an integration of many of the information gathering, processing, and analyzing functions under the impetus of the so-called systems approach. Such corporate territory has been, traditionally, the responsibility of the accountant and the financial man. It still is, to a large extent—but times are changing.

Does this, then, spell the early demise of the accountant as we know him today? Does it augur a lessening of influence for the financial specialists in today's corporate hierarchy? We think not. We maintain, however, that it is incumbent upon today's accountant and today's financial man to learn *today's* thinking and to *use today's* skills. It is for this reason the Wiley Series on Systems and Controls for Financial Management is being developed.

Recognizing the broad spectrum of interests and activites that the series title encompasses, we plan a number of volumes, each representing the latest thinking, written by a recognized authority, on a particular facet of the financial man's responsibilities. The subjects contemplated for discussion within the series range from production accounting systems to planning, to corporate records, to control of cash. Each book is an in-depth study of one subject within this group. Each is intended to be a practical, working tool for the businessman in general and the financial man and accountant in particular.

ROBERT L. SHULTIS

FRANK M. MASTROMANO

PREFACE

The most significant development in management accounting methodology in the last thirty years is the application of direct costing concepts to management planning and control problems. The significance of this development can be judged by the heat of the controversy it has generated and by the volume of literature praising or damning the technique. Yet nowhere in the vast volume of literature on the subject of direct costing has there appeared a thorough discussion of the application of this concept to planning and controlling expenses in all aspects of business operations. This book shows how direct costing can be applied to planning and controlling costs in production, marketing, and administrative functions within an organization.

This book is directed to the needs of the financial manager, accountant, or systems analyst who is looking for a detailed description of direct costing concepts and techniques and of the many analytical tools, such as cost–volume–profit analysis and contribution analysis, available for use with this system. It will also serve the manager who is confronted with a direct cost system for the first time or who wants to participate in the development of such a system. In addition, advanced students of accounting and management will find this book helpful as a reference work on direct cost and contribution accounting.

The book is divided into two parts. The first part emphasizes the role of direct cost and contribution data in an integrated management accounting system. The second part explores the techniques of analysis that draw on the data collected by the direct cost and contribution system.

Chapters 1 through 7 deal with the basic framework for an integrated management accounting system that is based on direct cost and contribution accounting concepts. The role of cost behavior analyses (Chapters 2 and 3) in the system is explained, and a methodology for identifying and measuring cost behavior patterns is described and illustrated. This illustration of cost behavior analysis is carried forward to the discussion of product costing to show how the results of cost behavior analysis are incorporated into the unit product cost.

Chapter 6 demonstrates how the same data can be used for developing segment performance reports for production segments of the firm. This chapter also draws on the concepts of responsibility accounting (Chapter 4) to reveal how company costs that are affected by a manager's decisions are charged to him, regardless of the functional unit in which the cost occurs.

Chapter 7 completes the management accounting system with a discussion of a contribution reporting system for the marketing function. The data from the previous chapters are incorporated into this chapter to focus on the multiple purposes for which data in a direct cost system can be used.

Chapters 8 through 11 are devoted to topics such as cost–volume–profit analysis and pricing decision analysis. In each of the chapters on contribution analysis, the data that make up a part of the management accounting system are again used to emphasize that the direct cost and contribution accounting system provides a data base to serve all decision models for which internal historical economic data are relevant. Direct cost data are relevant for pricing, and several ways in which they are useful to pricing analyses are presented in Chapters 10 and 11.

The importance of direct cost systems for service companies is discussed in Chapter 12. Although such companies do not produce a physical product that can be inventoried, this chapter shows how they can benefit significantly from direct cost and contribution information.

The impact of accounting information on human behavior is examined in Chapter 13, which indicates an approach to the design of accounting reports that will secure for the accountant the recipient behavior he wants. Accounting reports do not "just present the facts," and the accountant must recognize that what he puts in a report and the way he structures his report are critical to the effectiveness of the report. Chapter 13 does not tell the accountant how to appreciate human behavior in organizations; it tells him how to influence it with his reports.

Many people have contributed to this book. I have learned a great deal from the accountants and businessmen whom I have been privileged to instruct in executive development programs. However, I especially want to acknowledge the contributions of Arthur V. Corr of the National Association of Accountants and Walter B. McFarland of California State College, Hayward. Both of them taught me to appreciate the importance of direct cost information to management decisions.

GERMAIN BÖER

Stillwater, Oklahoma
December 1973

CONTENTS

CHAPTER 1

A DECISION FRAMEWORK
FOR DIRECT COSTING

Direct costing and contribution reporting provide the key to successful profit planning and control. These techniques supply business managers with the information needed for rational economic decisions. Information on production department performance, sales territory performance, and product performance is clearly set forth in monthly performance reports. Planning information in the form of direct standard product costs, direct fixed costs of marketing territories, and direct costs of service department activities is readily available for fast preparation of budget plans. Because direct costing and contribution reporting are such an integral part of effective planning and control systems, the characteristics of planning and control are examined in the next few paragraphs to provide a clear perspective on their meaning.

PLANNING AND CONTROL

In a study on *long-range profit planning* by the National Association of Accountants, the planning process is defined as " . . . a systematic and formalized process for purposefully directing and controlling future operations toward desired objectives for periods extending beyond one year."* The plan that results from this process includes a statement of objectives and a formal program of intended action which usually takes the form of a budget.

   Managers use forecasts of revenues, economic conditions, and costs in constructing a budget plan, but planning and forecasting differ significantly

* *Long-Range Profit Planning*, Research Report 42 New York: National Association of Accountants, 1964, p. 4.

in meaning. A business that plans for the future actively tries to direct its growth toward a specific objective; a business that merely forecasts the future passively predicts what might happen and then waits to see what does happen. In such a business, managers make no attempt to influence the environment in which the business operates. Instead, managers devote their energies to keeping score on the number of times they guessed correctly. Even though a company uses the most sophisticated computerized forecasting models to develop its predictions, company managers are planning only if they take positive steps to guide the direction in which the company is moving.

The program of intended action developed in the planning process plays a significant role in control activities. In fact, no process, revenue, or cost can be controlled unless actual results can be compared with some standard that was developed as part of the planning process. A production manager determines whether his costs are out of control by comparing actual cost with a standard, or budgeted, cost. A marketing manager ascertains whether territory contribution is adequate by relating actual territory contribution to a budgeted, or planned, amount. The director of a research program checks to see that his costs are under control by comparing his planned costs with his actual expenditures. In other words, without planning there is no control.

The concept of control involves more than just comparing actual results and plans. Thousands of companies prepare reports comparing actual costs and planned costs without controlling any costs. The action taken by the department head, the sales manager, or the research director is the critical link in the control process. If the production supervisor, when he receives his performance report, turns it over and uses the back side for scratch paper, costs are not controlled. If the territory manager ignores his monthly performance report, sales territory contribution is not controlled, even though elaborate comparisons of planned and actual territory contribution are developed. Thus, although control involves a comparison of actual results to the plan, effective control requires positive action to keep the two together.

DECISION MAKING

The planning and control processes utilize direct cost information as the raw material for profit planning decisions and cost control decisions. Accordingly, decision making is examined in the next few pages to provide an insight into the kinds of decisions made within an organization and to identify the types of decisions that benefit from direct cost information. Decisions are examined in terms of organizational levels and in terms of the time period affected by the decision.

In every decision situation, a manager chooses a course of action from among several alternatives. The president of a conglomerate selects an acquisition strategy from several alternative strategies; the advertising manager for a food products company chooses a level of advertising expenditure from several alternative spending levels; the production supervisor selects the quantity of raw material required for a batch of units entering his production process. In each of these cases, the decision maker selects an alternative from the various ones available. However, the impact on the organization and the information requirements of each of these decisions differ. The differences among the decisions are clearly set out in the decision hierarchy developed by Robert Anthony.*

This three-level decision hierarchy consists of strategic planning decisions (roughly, top management decisons), management control decisions (roughly, middle management decisions), and operational control decisions (roughly, operating management decisions). Strategic planning decisions are concerned with decisions that are usually made at the top levels in the organization. Decisions on acquisition strategy, organization goals, and broad company policies are made at this level. Decisions that fall in this category usually affect the entire organization or large segments of the organization. For instance, a decision by a toy manufacturer with headquarters in Chicago to shift its production facilities to Dallas fits the strategic planning decision category. Large capital expenditure proposals also rank in the strategic planning decision group.

One of the major characteristics of strategic planning decisions is the lack of explicit decision models. No decision model can tell the president of a department store chain whether he should become a conglomerate and begin to purchase banks and farm equipment manufacturing companies. Numerous factors influence the president's decision, and most of these factors are subjective. In addition, the information used in strategic planning decisions usually originates outside the business. New product possibilities, potential acquisitions, and marketing strategies are customarily developed as a result of information about economic conditions and competitive activity. Monthly accounting reports are relatively insignificant inputs for the strategic planning decision.

However, management control decisions rely heavily on accounting techniques for planning and control. The management control decision cate-

* Robert N. Anthony, *Planning and Control Systems: A Framework for Analysis,* Division of Research Graduate School of Business Administration, Harvard University, Cambridge, Mass., 1965.

gory includes those decisions that operate within the framework established by the strategic planning decions. For example, if a strategic planning decision establishes a company objective of an annual profit growth of 10%, the management control decisions will select activities that lead to the attainment of this objective. Stated another way, the strategic planning decisions determine the boundaries within which management control decisions are made.

Also, management control decisions are involved with optimizing current operations, whereas strategic planning decisions focus on the shape of the organization in which the management control decisions are made. Preparing the annual budget, controlling production costs, determining the most profitable product mix, all are management control decisions made within the framework established by a strategic planning decision.

Psychological considerations are important in management control decisions. Effective sales budgets are prepared by consulting the salesman who is later asked to attain the budgeted sales, and production personnel participate in the preparation of production cost budgets and standards. Cost control requires managers to work through other managers, as well as employees, to keep actual costs equal to planned costs.

The information used in management control decisions consists of both external and internal information. External information is significant for planning decisions. For instance, managers need information about competitors, customers, and economic conditions to prepare the annual sales budget. Internally generated information on productive capacity and marketing capacity is also important in developing the annual sales budget. On the other hand, information for control decisions at the management control level comes almost entirely from within the firm. Monthly performance reports compare actual costs with standard costs and planned segment contribution to actual segment contribution. Data for these reports are generated from information stored in data files within the company.

Just as management control decisions are constrained by decisions made at the strategic planning level, operational control decisions are limited by decisions made at the management control level. The maker of operational control decisions is concerned with assuring that specific tasks are carried out properly. Such decisions are highly structured and involve production scheduling, inventory reordering, and payroll preparation; decisions that can be described in a procedures manual or programmed on a computer are operational control decisions.

Inventory management decisions provide an example of the difference between management control and operational control decisions. Selecting a customer service level and selecting the specific technique for controlling various inventory items are management control decisions. Reordering inventory when the reorder point is reached for an item or choosing the economic order quantity from a reorder table are operational control decisions. The reorder decision and the quantity decision require no judgment on the part of the operational control decision maker; the management control decision maker exercised his judgment when he selected the underlying factors that resulted in the reorder point and the economic order quantity table.

Operational control decisions require a high volume of information that frequently consists of nonmonetary data. Information on hours worked, pounds of material used, and feet of material wasted provide the data input for operational control decisions. Information for such decisions deals with specific items or transactions; almost no summarized information is used.

Mathematical decision models and computerized decision making are useful for operational control decisions because the decisions are structured. The economic order quantity is automatically computed once all the inputs to the model have been specified, and the optimum product mix is determined by a linear programming model once the variables needed for the computation have been named. Both the inventory decision and the product mix decision are improved by the mathematical formulation of the decision because no judgment is required in these decisions.

In addition to considering the hierarchical nature of business decisions, a manager can also view decisions from the standpoint of the time period affected by the decision (i.e., long-range planning versus short-range planning and control decisions). Long-range planning decisions are concerned with the future effects of present decisions.* These decisions consider how construction of an automated factory affects production capacity 10 to 15 years in the future. Long-range planning decisions determine production and marketing capacity by developing a timetable for increasing or decreasing these capacities.

Short-range planning and control decisions are concerned primarily with utilizing as efficiently as possible the capacity provided by the long-range decisions.In short-range planning and control decisions, capacity is an unchangeable constraint on operations. The plant manager in planning his operations for a one-year period attempts to operate his existing plant with maximum efficiency; the marketing manager in his one-year plan attempts to maximize the contribution of his segment to company profits. Neither the plant manager nor the marketing manager considers the effects of capacity changes as he develops his annual budget.

The three-level decision hierarchy and the time period approach to

---

* Peter F. Drucker, "Long-Range Planning: Challenge to Management Science," *Management Science*, 5 (April 1959), pp. 238–249.

business decisions are interrelated. Long-range planning decisions are similar to strategic planning decisions in that both decisions affect business capacity. However, long-range planning decisions focus on the development of plans for a specific time period, whereas the dominant characteristic of the strategic planning decision is its impact on the organization. Strategic planning decisions may require a long period of time for implementation, but the implementation of the strategic planning decision requires management control decisions. The distinction between long-range planning decisions and strategic planning decisions is best summarized by noting that long-range planning decisions focus only on the time period affected by the decision, whereas strategic planning decisions include several factors in addition to the time dimension.

The management control decisions frequently correspond to short-range planning decisions. Both decisions are involved with utilizing existing capacity, and both are concerned with ongoing business activities. Both decisions include such activities as annual profit planning and monthly performance evaluation. However, management control decisions can also be long-range planning decisions for those cases in which the long-range plan is a program for utilizing existing capacity. Only when the long-range plan calls for changes in capacity does this decision fit the strategic planning decision category. The short-range decisions and management control decisions differ in that the short-range decisions concentrate on the time span affected by the decision, whereas management control decisions include numerous other factors.

A DECISION FRAMEWORK FOR DIRECT COSTING

Before setting forth the decision framework on which the remainder of this book is based, some terms are defined. A direct cost, as used in this book, is a cost that is traceable to an object, activity, organizational segment, or individual. Cost behavior is independent of the "directness" of a cost. Therefore, fixed costs as well as variable costs are direct costs.

Marginal income is the difference between revenue and the direct variable costs. Contribution is the dollar amount remaining after direct fixed costs have been deducted from marginal income. The following example illustrates the meaning of these terms.

Example Company produces a product called Ixnay that is sold in three marketing territories (North, South, East). The standard direct cost of producing Ixnay is $5 per unit, and the normal selling price is $10. During March the Northern territory compiled the following data:

Sales   20,000 units @$10

Costs of operating territory
    Territory manager salary $ 2,000
    Territory office expense   4,000
    Five salesmen @$2,000   10,000
    Sales commissions 3% of sales

The data were used to prepare the following report.

Example Company
Territory Contribution Report for the Month of March

Sales		$200,000
Variable production costs	$100,000	
Variable marketing costs	6,000	106,000
Marginal income		$ 94,000
Direct fixed costs		
Territory manager	$ 2,000	
Territory office expense	4,000	
Salesmen salaries	10,000	16,000
Contribution		$ 78,000

In this example, the direct costs of the sales consist of both production costs and marketing costs totaling $106,000. These direct variable costs are deducted from total revenue of $200,000 for a marginal income amount of $94,000. Deducting the direct fixed costs of the Northern territory from the marginal income provides a territory contribution of $78,000.

Direct cost and contribution information are more useful for some decisions than for others. Direct cost information is extremely valuable for management control decisions that relate to short-term planning periods, and it is used to some extent in long-range decisions that extend over several years. Strategic planning decisions receive some benefit from direct cost information, but the importance of direct cost information for these decisions is minor compared with its significance for management control decisions. Operational control decisions are relatively unaffected by direct cost information, since these decisions usually exclude monetary information. Direct costing concepts are useful in capacity decisions, but the concepts are already incorporated in the assumptions underlying capital expenditure planning techniques. The relation of direct cost information to the various decision categories is summarized in Figure 1–1.

Direct cost information provides relevant data for planning activities in cost segments of the business by showing the cost effect of various levels of

A Decision Framework for Direct Costing

Type of Decision	Impact on Decision of Direct Cost Information
Strategic planning	Minor
Management control	Significant
Operational control	Minor
Long-range planning	Moderate
Short-range planning	Significant

Figure 1-1

activity in each segment. A direct cost system shows the cost change in production department costs for increases or decreases in production output. Revenue generating segment plans are improved with direct cost information by highlighting the impact on contribution of changes in prices, promotion costs, and other selling costs direct to the revenue generating segment. The segment contribution reflects activities originating in and controlled by the revenue generating segment. No arbitrary cost allocations distort the segment contribution and confuse the planning decisions related to the revenue generating segment.

Control decisions for cost segments of the firm are improved because only the costs that an individual can influence are reported to him. No overhead expense is charged to a production supervisor unless he influences the overhead expense with his decisions. Consequently, when a performance report for a department indicates that a cost is out of control, the supervisor of that department has the decision making power to bring the cost under control.

Control of revenue generating segments focuses on the decisions that affect segment contribution. The objective in control decisions for revenue generating segments is not cost minimization but contribution maximization. If a sales manager can increase his contribution by spending more than the budgeted amount for advertising, the direct cost control report will emphasize the increased contribution instead of the cost variance.

CHAPTER 2

COST CONCEPTS AND COST BEHAVIOR

Cost concepts are relevant only if they influence a decision, and cost data are relevant only if they are useful to a cost concept. For example, unit product cost concepts are useful for decisions on product profitability, but they are useless for cost control decisions. Moreover, the data accumulated to develop unit product costs can be assembled using either a direct cost concept or an absorption cost concept. Direct cost data are relevant for planning decisions that use product cost information, but absorption cost data are useful only for external reporting purposes. Accordingly, the accountant should be aware of several cost concepts if he is to design an effective direct cost system.

COST CONCEPTS

Traceable Costs

Some of the cost concepts that are useful in developing a direct cost system are: traceable costs, common costs, and opportunity costs. A traceable cost (also called a separable cost) is directly related to a unit of a product, a department, or a sales territory. The material cost of a unit of product, the labor cost of a unit of product, and the variable overhead in a unit of product are all costs that are traceable to the unit of product. The administrative salaries, the rent, and the supplies expense of a district sales office are traceable to that sales district. These costs are direct costs of the district sales office. In fact, direct costs and traceable costs are interchangeable terms.

Common Costs

Common costs, on the other hand, support a number of activities or organization segments. The monthly fixed costs of operating a production de-

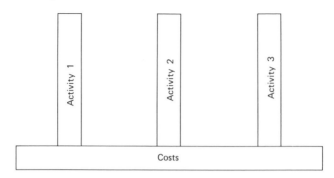

Figure 2-1

partment are common to all units produced by that department during the month. The cost of administration in the New York sales district is common to all units of product sold in that territory. A common cost does not change even when one of the activities it supports is discontinued. For instance, the monthly administration costs of the New York sales district will remain constant even if one of the products currently being sold in that district is discontinued. The same is true for a production department that works on several products; eliminating one of the products will not eliminate the common fixed costs of operating the department.

In Figure 2-1, any of the three activities can be eliminated or changed with no effect on the common costs. The common costs remain to support activities 1 and 2 if activity 3 is eliminated, and they remain to support activities 2 and 3 if activity 1 is eliminated. However, the common costs in Figure 2-1 are not inherently common because of the nature of the cost. These common costs are traceable costs if the three activities are viewed as one activity. The departmental production costs that are common to all the units produced in a department are direct costs of the total units produced during any one month. For example, assume that Production Department 426 performs the final assembly work on the Quick Cutter lawn mower manufactured by Lawnmower, Inc. The supervisory costs and certain other fixed costs of this department are common to each of the individual lawn mowers assembled in this department during July. However, in evaluating the profitability of the Quick Cutter, the company managers consider the same costs to be direct costs of producing the Quick Cutter mowers.

Consequently, whether a cost is direct or common depends on the decision for which the cost is relevant. The unit direct cost of the Quick Cutter mower is relevant for short-term pricing decisions during periods of low production activity, but the departmental direct fixed cost of producing the

Quick Cutter is relevant for long-term pricing decisions. Another factor affecting the designation of a cost as common or direct is the perspective of the decision maker. In Figure 2-1, for example, the supervisor who is in charge of activity 3 considers the costs supporting the three activities to be common costs. However, the supervisor in charge of all three activities considers the same costs to be direct (or traceable) costs of his area of responsibility.

Opportunity Cost

Besides being concerned with the traceability of costs, the accountant must recognize the concept of opportunity cost. Opportunity cost is the marginal income or contribution that is given up because one alternative is chosen in preference to another. This concept, which centers on foregone opportunities instead of cash expenditures, is relevant for those decisions in which a scarce resource must be utilized as efficiently as possible. For example, product mix decisions for a machine that is producing at full capacity are based on the marginal income per hour earned from the products that can be produced on the machine. If a manager chooses to produce a product with less than the highest marginal income per hour, the marginal income earned per hour will be less than the marginal income per hour foregone. In other words, the hourly marginal income foregone (opportunity cost) will exceed the hourly marginal income earned.

COST BEHAVIOR

In addition to considering the cost concept that is relevant for a particular decision, the accountant must bear in mind the relation of cost changes to changes in activity levels. Information about costs that change with changes in activity levels and those that do not is essential for sound planning decisions. A manager selects a course of action by examining the costs of the alternatives available to him. He must know what levels of cost to expect for different activity levels if he is to develop a plan of action to meet his profit objective. This means that the accountant must provide an analysis of costs in terms of their behavior patterns; that is, the cost per unit of activity and the cost per time period must be readily available for making cost projections for alternative courses of action.

Knowledge of cost behavior patterns is also critical for cost control decisions because costs can be controlled only if the accountant can compute the level of cost that the company should have incurred for the actual

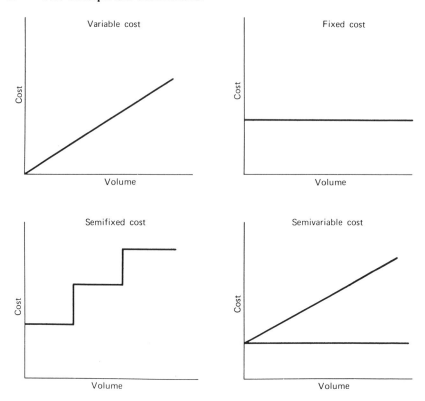

Figure 2-2   Cost behavior patterns.

volume of work performed in a department during a specific time period. For instance, the budgeted cost level in a production department for January is related both to the number of units produced during January and to the passage of one month. These budgeted costs can be computed if costs have been classified according to their variability in relation to output and to the passage of time.

Cost Behavior Patterns

Changes in activity and the passage of time are the two factors that determine the behavior patterns of costs. Costs such as material and labor change as the level of production changes, but administrative salaries vary with the passage of time. Costs that vary directly with changes in activity are called variable costs, and those that vary with the passage of time are called fixed costs. These costs are graphically illustrated in Figure 2-2.

The variable costs which are represented by a straight line drawn from the origin, include material, labor, variable overhead, sales commissions, and other costs that vary directly with changes in an activity level. The fixed costs are represented by a line drawn parallel to the horizontal axis. Costs such as administrative salaries, property taxes, lease contracts, and depreciation exhibit this type of behavior pattern.

The remaining two cost behavior patterns shown in Figure 2-2 are variations of the fixed and variable cost behavior patterns. Semivariable costs consist of both a base amount that remains constant in relation to activity changes and a portion that varies directly with changes in the activity level. Supplies expense for a production department reflects such behavior. A minimum amount of supplies is required in a production department to get activities started, and additional quantities of supplies are required as the level of output in the department increases. Compensation for a salesman who is paid a monthly salary plus a commission on his sales is also a semivariable cost.

Semifixed costs are sometimes called stair-step costs because of their graphical resemblance to stair steps. These costs consist of layers of fixed costs which are added as specific levels of volume are attained. They change in lump-sum amounts at certain levels of activity instead of changing continuously over all levels of activity. Many types of personnel costs fit this behavior pattern. Supervisory costs are frequently semifixed expenses because each supervisor is able to supervise a limited number of employees. As production increases to the point at which each supervisor is working at his limit, adding one more worker because of an increase in production requires one more supervisor. Other personnel costs, such as those in the billing department, may also follow a semifixed pattern.

In developing procedures for planning and controlling the various types of costs, the accountant must recognize that the behavior patterns of the costs hold true only for the relevant, or normal, range of activities. The cost behavior of material no longer follows a straight line if a production department operates at 150% of capacity, and fixed costs for a plant will shift upward if the plant operates far beyond its capacity. Also, the behavior of costs at very low levels of operation may differ from expectations. Labor cost may be variable within the normal range of activity for a plant, but at low levels of activity the labor cost may reach a lower fixed limit because of management reluctance to lose skilled workers.

The relevant range of activities normally consists of the range of activity within which a department expects to operate during the planning period. For example, the planned monthly production for a factory department may vary between 80 and 100% of one-shift capacity. The relevant range over which the accountant would analyze expenses is this expected range of production.

By defining a relatively narrow "relevant range" of activity for his cost analysis instead of considering the entire range of outputs possible for a department, the accountant also avoids the problems of curvilinear cost functions, which usually describe cost behavior for all possible levels of output. This is the cost curve that economists use to describe production costs for the firm. The curve rises sharply at low levels of production, rises more slowly over the middle levels of production, and rises sharply again at high levels of output.

The accountant can use a straight line to describe variable costs, for instance, because the relevant range restricts his analysis to a small part of the possible output represented by the economist's cost curve, and a small segment of the cost curve is very closely approximated by a straight line. The approximation is so close, in fact, that optimal short-term planning and control decisions can readily be made using the straight line assumption of cost behavior.

Variable Cost Determinants

No cost is inherently fixed or variable. Therefore, fixed and variable costs are examined further to point out some of the factors that cause expenses to behave as fixed or variable. Variable costs are incurred to utilize existing capacity to produce and sell goods. Material cost is a good example of a variable cost because it varies directly with changes in the level of production. However, such is not the case with expenses such as labor. Labor cost can be fixed or variable or any combination of the two, depending on how management decides the expense should behave. If management decides to maintain a stable labor force with no overtime work, labor cost is a fixed expense; if a stable labor force is maintained with overtime worked as needed, labor cost is fixed up to a point. Beyond that point the cost behaves like a semivariable cost.

The time span affected by a decision also influences the variability of a cost. Costs that are fixed for monthly planning decisions may be variable costs for decisions spanning a 2-year planning period. For example, a bank may find that personnel costs in one of its branches are constant throughout each month, but the same costs vary with deposit volume when a 2-year time period is considered. In this case, personnel costs are fixed for short-term planning and control decisions, but they are variable costs for long-range planning decisions.

Organization perspective, too, affects the variability of a cost. The supervisor of a production department considers the cost of heating or cooling his department to be a fixed cost because the cost is unaffected by changes in output of his department. In contrast, heating and cooling costs are variable costs from the viewpoint of the manager in charge of providing these services. Since his costs fluctuate with the amount of heating or cooling his department produces, he considers them to be variable costs. In general, a cost is a variable cost of a department if the cost changes because of a change in activity in that department.

A cost may be fixed from the total company viewpoint, but the same cost may be variable from a departmental perspective. Consider maintenance costs as an illustration of this situation. A company may support a fixed staff in its maintenance department regardless of the fluctuations in demand for maintenance services. At the same time, the company may charge individual departments for the use of maintenance services in such a manner that maintenance cost is a variable cost to the using department. In this case, a cost that is fixed from the total organization perspective is variable from an organization segment viewpoint. Companies treat maintenance cost, or any other cost, in this manner to try to reduce total cost. By making maintenance cost a variable cost to the using departments, the company creates a decision environment in which departmental managers can influence departmental maintenance costs in the short run. Ideally such a procedure will result in cost minimization in all using departments, which in turn will reduce total company costs.

By converting maintenance cost into a variable cost for individual departments, the company increases the frequency with which departmental managers make decisions that affect maintenance cost. This increased decision frequency is not true of variable maintenance cost only; all decisions affecting variable costs are made at frequent intervals. Every time a production worker decides how to place a piece of metal in a stamping machine, his decision affects the cost of material used in his department. The supervisory decisions a departmental manager makes every day influence the labor costs of his department. Most of the decisions made by operating managers and production personnel on a day-to-day basis directly affect variable costs.

Decisions that affect variable costs are usually in the management control or operational control decision categories, and the results of such decisions are evident shortly after a decision has been made. Strategic planning decisions may set the general level of variable costs by specifying the degree of automation in a plant, for example; but short-range planning and control decisions directly affect the actual level of variable costs that occur in the plant. Strategic planning and certain types of management control decisions (e.g., training policy decisions) indirectly influence variable costs; but the direct month-to-month impact on variable costs results from short-range operational control and management control decisions.

Fixed Cost Determinants

Fixed costs, in contrast, are affected by long-range management control planning decisions and by strategic planning decisions. The strategic planning decisions that determine production and marketing capacity occur at relatively infrequent intervals, whereas the management control decisions resulting in fixed costs occur frequently. The difference in decision level and frequency results in two kinds of fixed costs: committed fixed costs and planned fixed costs.*

1. *Committed fixed costs* result from decisions to acquire productive capacity. Long-term lease commitments and depreciation costs tend to remain constant for long periods of time, and these costs change when a decision is made to change capacity.

2. *Planned fixed costs* result from decisions on staff levels, levels of advertising expenditure, research expenditure levels, and so on. Decisions affecting these costs are usually made annually, and the costs can be increased or decreased in the short run.

The committed fixed costs originate in plant capacity decisions, and the planned fixed costs originate in decisions on the use of that capacity. Advertising expense is a planned fixed cost, incurred by a company to generate a sales volume that allows its plants to operate at efficient levels. Planned expenditures on sales personnel are made for the same reason. Staff levels in administrative functions are planned fixed costs, and the level of these costs is planned by considering the number of personnel required to perform the planned level of work. Consequently, managers can increase planned fixed costs whenever they decide to do so.

The relevant level of fixed expense is different for different decisions. For example, shutdown fixed costs are usually lower than the operating fixed costs of a plant. The shutdown fixed cost level is relevant for planning decisions involving plant shutdowns, and the operating fixed costs are relevant for planning and control decisions related to utilizing the plant efficiently. Short-range pricing decisions during periods of excess capacity frequently ignore fixed costs, but long-range pricing policy must consider expected future levels of fixed costs.

* National Association of Accountants, *The Analysis of Cost-Volume-Profit Relationships*, Research Reports 16, 17, and 18, (New York: National Association of Accountants, 1950), pp. 1–6.

Another consideration influencing fixed expenses is the degree of traceability of a fixed cost to a specific time period.* Administrative salaries are direct costs of the time period in which they are paid, and lease payments are direct costs of the time period in which they are paid. Other fixed costs, however, are incurred in a lump-sum amount for capacity that will be used over a series of future time periods. The lump-sum amount is a common cost to all the periods benefiting from the expenditure, and any apportionment of this cost to an individual time period is arbitrary.

The apportionment of this common cost to specific time periods usually takes the form of depreciation expense—an expense that varies with the computational procedure selected by a company. Because selection of a depreciation method is a subjective judgment, no single depreciation method is correct. Accordingly, the subjective nature of depreciation costs should be clearly identified in monthly performance reports, to allow managers to see readily the irrelevance of depreciation expense for planning decisions. (It is irrelevant because it provides no information to a manager for choosing among alternatives.) Since depreciation expense is used to compute periodic net income, monthly income statements should include a separate section in which period cost allocations are specifically identified, thus emphasizing the subjective nature of these expense amounts. Fortunately, the degree of subjectivity decreases as the time span covered by a report increases. Annual profit figures are less subjective than monthly amounts, and a 5-year net profit amount is less subjective than an annual profit amount.†

Besides considering the traceability of a fixed cost to a time period, the accountant must consider the viewpoint of the decision maker who will use the cost information. Department supervisors will consider many costs fixed that a plant manager considers semifixed or variable because the department supervisor considers as fixed all costs unaffected by his decisions. Yet many of the costs unaffected by decisions at the department level are planned and controlled at the plant manager level. Fewer costs are fixed at higher levels in the organization because the time horizon of a top-level manager stretches far into the future, which means that almost all costs can change with changes in company activity.

Planning and Controlling Costs

Although costs do not display a specific behavior pattern because of their nature, behavior pattern identification is essential for effective cost plan-

* National Association of Accountants, *Accounting for Costs of Capacity*, Research Report 39, (New York: National Association of Accountants, May 1963), pp. 35–37.
† Edward G. Nelson, "The Relation Between the Balance Sheet and the Profit-and-Loss Statement," *The Accounting Review,* 17 (April 1942), pp. 132–141.

ning and control. Variable costs are planned by applying unit variable costs to the forecast volume of activity. Material cost is planned by considering the quantity and price of material needed for production; variable overhead expense is planned by computing the dollar amount of overhead required for the planned production; and variable labor cost is planned by developing the quantity and rate of labor necessary for the planned production. Variable costs are controlled by comparing actual variable cost for a department with the budgeted variable cost that should have been incurred for the actual department output. The budgeted cost is computed by multiplying unit variable cost elements by actual production. Actual material cost charged to a department is then compared with budgeted material cost for the actual production volume attained in that department.

Planning fixed costs differs according to whether committed or planned fixed cost are involved. Formal procedures and formal decision models are very significant for committed fixed cost planning because of the long time interval between such decisions. Moreover, decisions that generate committed fixed costs affect the company for many years into the future; thus a long-range plan is an essential part of committed fixed cost planning. Since a decision today to expand plant capacity influences what the company will be like 10 years from now, a manager cannot make a sound decision today unless he knows what he wants the company to be like a decade hence. The control of committed fixed costs occurs simultaneously with the planning of the fixed cost, since that is the point in time at which the future level of the committed fixed cost is set.

Planned fixed costs, in contrast, are usually developed as part of the annual profit plan. The sales budget and the level of advertising and promotion costs are planned simultaneously. Staff levels in various administrative departments are planned by considering the number of personnel required to handle the planned volume of activty for the coming year. Control of planned fixed costs is accomplished through monthly or quarterly budget reports in which planned expense for the period is compared with actual cost.

Semifixed costs may be planned and controlled like variable costs or like planned fixed costs. They are treated like variable costs if the steps are so small that a straight line approximates the step cost function. For relatively large steps (i.e., costs remain constant over wide ranges of volume), the costs are treated like planned fixed costs except that the year is broken into weeks, months, or quarters for cost planning. A planning budget showing the expense levels for various ranges of volume provides dollar amounts for planning expense levels for different volumes of activity. The same budget is later used to compute budgeted expense for comparison with actual cost.

Semivariable costs, because they are partly fixed and partly variable, are planned and controlled in two parts. The variable portion of the expense is planned and controlled like a variable cost, and the fixed portion (in most cases) is treated like a planned fixed cost.

COST BEHAVIOR ANALYSIS

One of the first tasks faced by the accountant attempting to install a direct cost system is the classification of costs into the four behavior patterns mentioned earlier in the chapter. This classification process is actually a two-step procedure involving (1) the identification of expense behavior and (2) dollar measurement of the cost for use in planning and control decisions. The remainder of this chapter is devoted to identification of behavior patterns; cost measurement is taken up in Chapter 3.

Identifying Cost Behavior Patterns

All costs incurred by a business result from decisions made by individuals in the organization. The type and dollar amount of the cost are then recorded in the accounting records as illustrated in Figure 2-3. To determine how a cost behaves, the accountant can begin either at the left side of Figure 2-3 (decision maker) or at the right side (accounting records).

If he begins his analysis with the decision maker, he utilizes interviews with department heads throughout the company to determine how costs behave in each department. Data from these interviews are collected on a *cost behavior identification work sheet* like the one illustrated in Figure 2-4. On the left side of this work sheet, expenses influenced by the departmental supervisor's decisions are listed, and columns for the four behavior patterns are placed to the right of the expenses. The accountant discusses the behavior of each cost with the department supervisor to determine how

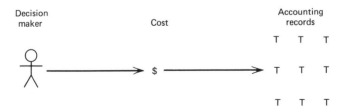

Figure 2-3   Decision–cost relationship.

Department: _____

Supervisor: _____

Expense	Variable		Semivariable		Semifixed		Fixed
	√	Varies with	√	Varies with	√	Varies with	
Direct material							
Direct labor							
Supervision							
Indirect labor							
Supplies							
Maintenance							
Power and light							

Figure 2-4   Cost behavior identification sheet

the cost behaves and to ascertain whether the department manager actually does make decisions that influence the level of the cost. Department managers may have no understanding of cost behavior patterns, but they will know whether more labor is used as production increases or whether the quantity of supplies used fluctuates with changes in production.

Another advantage of the interview technique is that it permits the identification of departmental costs that vary with different causal factors. For example, material cost in a production department may vary directly with total units produced by the production department, but power costs of the department may vary directly with machine hours. In this case, the two costs could be planned and controlled by using two different activity measures.

If the accountant attempts to identify cost behavior patterns by analyzing data in the accounting records, he assumes that the results of decisions are accurately reflected in the data that describe the events produced by the decisions. This approach usually relies on statistical techniques, such as correlation analysis and least squares regression procedures (the least squares technique is illustrated in the next chapter). These techniques attempt to measure the change in an expense in relation to changes in activity. For example, changes in labor cost are measured in relation to changes in output in a production department to determine whether labor cost in that department is fixed, variable, or semivariable. Semifixed costs

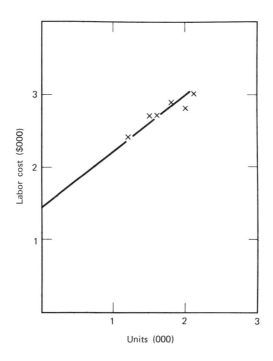

Month	Units	Labor Cost
January	1,600	$2,700
February	1,800	2,900
March	2,100	3,000
April	2,000	2,800
May	1,500	2,700
June	1,200	2,400

Figure 2-5   Cost–output relationship.

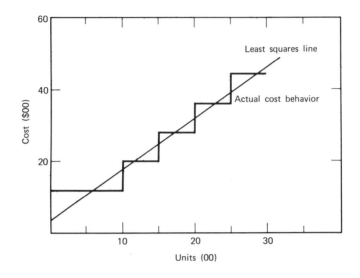

I. Budgetary data

Monthly Activity Range (units)	Monthly Budgeted Cost
0–1,000	$1,200
1,001–1,500	2,000
1,501–2,000	2,800
2,001–2,500	3,600
2,501–3,000	4,400

II. Data from operations

Month	Units Produced	Actual Expense
January	1,100	$2,000
February	1,400	2,000
March	1,700	2,800
April	2,100	4,400
May	2,600	4,400
June	2,400	3,600

Figure 2-6 Regression analysis of a semifixed cost.

22

cannot be identified from data analysis; interview techniques must be used to identify these costs.

The basic idea of the data analysis approach to cost behavior identification is illustrated in Figure 2-5, where the cost amounts for various levels of output are plotted on a graph. A straight line is drawn through the points, and the slope of the line indicates the behavior pattern of the cost being analyzed. In Figure 2-5 the slope of the line reveals that the cost is a semivariable cost, since the line specifies a positive cost at zero output. A variable cost of course, would be described by an upward sloping line from the origin, and a fixed cost would be described by a straight line parallel to the horizontal axis. The reader can refer to any basic statistics book for a detailed discussion of the techniques of correlation analysis.

Before he decides to use this approach to behavior analysis, however, the accountant should be aware of the limitations and assumptions of these techniques.* First of all, data analysis presumes that accurate cost and output records are available for a number of past time periods (e.g., detailed cost records by department on a weekly or monthly basis for the past year.) If the past data are available, any unusual fluctuations they contain must be removed before the statistical techniques are applied. Moreover, a basic assumption of these methods is that the process that generated the historical data being analyzed is the same one that will be experienced in the future—that is, production methods will remain the same, the same materials will be used in the product, and prices paid for cost elements will remain constant.

Another problem relates to the recording procedures used for costs and output. If departmental production is recorded in the week it occurs and labor costs are recorded as they are paid, there will be a lag between the change in production and the change in labor cost. Likewise, if the total material cost of a batch of product is charged to a department at the start of the production process and material is issued to the department as needed, material cost and production levels will not be recorded in the same time period.

Semifixed costs present a problem if the data analysis approach to cost behavior identification is used. The problem arises because the statistical techniques presume that costs change continuously over all ranges of activity, but semifixed costs do not behave in this manner. Yet because semifixed costs do change as volume changes, statistical regression analysis interprets the change as a continuous one. Figure 2-6 illustrates the kind of results that might be provided by a least squares analysis of a

* George Benston, "Multiple Regression Analysis of Cost Behavior," *The Accounting Review,* **41** (October 1966), pp. 657–672.

semifixed cost. In this illustration, the stair-step pattern accurately reflects the behavior of the cost. The straight line represents the result of a least squares analysis of the data used to plot the semifixed cost. The least squares analysis indicates that the cost is a semivariable cost even though the cost is a semifixed cost. Consequently, data analysis techniques do not afford a means of identifying semifixed costs.

CHAPTER 3

COST ANALYSIS AND FLEXIBLE OVERHEAD BUDGETS

We dealt with cost behavior and the identification of cost behavior patterns in Chapter 2, and the discussion is continued in this chapter. First, measurement of the dollar amounts of various expenses is examined; then the development of flexible overhead budgets is explored.

COST MEASUREMENT

Cost measurement, the second stage in the process of cost behavior analysis, normally occurs after cost behavior patterns have been identified (see Chapter 2). Cost measurement is essential for the direct cost system because the accountant needs dollar values for the various costs in order to compute budget amounts for planning and control. Therefore, any procedure that the accountant uses to measure a cost must incorporate the expected cost level for the planning period during which that cost will be incurred. Historical costs may be helpful in arriving at dollar values for the various costs, but the dollar amounts included in budgets and standards must reflect future cost levels and not past cost levels.

Variable Costs

Cost measurements for variable costs may be developed in several ways. One method requires the departmental foreman or cost analyst to estimate the dollar increase in cost for changes in activity. This procedure has the advantage of low cost and fast answers, but it also has the disadvantages that are associated with personal estimates of dollar costs. When using personal estimates to develop unit variable costs, the accountant should always

Computing Unit Variable Cost

1. Historical data

Month	Material Cost	Units Produced
January	$ 8,840	4,200
February	8,300	4,000
March	8,100	4,100
April	6,860	3,500
May	6,380	3,200
June	6,180	3,000
Totals	$44,660	22,000

2. Average unit variable cost
   Average material cost per unit = $44,660/22,000 = $2.03
3. Unit variable cost for budgetary use
   Average material cost per unit $2.03
   Expected material price increase for coming year   .47

   Budgeted unit variable cost $2.50

Figure 3-1

verify the reasonableness of the cost estimate by applying the unit cost estimate to output for a prior period. If there is a significant difference
between the prior period cost and the one calculated using the estimate, the
accountant should have the foreman or department head reconsider his
original estimate, or another procedure should be used to develop the cost
estimate.

As an alternative, variable cost can be estimated by computing an
average of the cost for a past period after which the average is adjusted for
future factors that affect the cost. Figure 3-1 illustrates this approach to
computing unit variable cost. In this example the variable costs incurred
and units produced are accumulated for a 6-month period. The total cost is
divided by the total units to arrive at a $2.03 average unit variable cost for
the 6-month period. This average is adjusted upward for expected price
increases averaging $.47 per unit, resulting in a budgeted unit variable cost
of $2.50. This cost can be further adjusted for changes in production
methods, changes in quality of ..aterial, changes in the quality of personnel, and so forth. All these adjustments are made to develop a

measurement of variable cost that will reasonably approximate the unit variable cost expected during the coming year, the coming quarter, or whatever planning period the company uses.

Fixed Costs

Fixed cost measurement techniques vary with the type of fixed cost. Committed fixed cost values are usually taken from the general ledger in which expenses such as depreciation are recorded. Future expense amounts are then determined by adjusting the past amounts upward or downward for assets that will be acquired or sold during the planning period.

The planned fixed cost values are derived by referring to general ledger amounts, by examining budgeted amounts for the planning period, and by discussing spending plans with the executives who set the level of the planned fixed cost. Because planned fixed cost levels are determined by considering the expected future volume of business, it is important to dis-

Computing Semifixed Cost Values

1. Historical data

Week	Number of Supervisors	Weekly Supervisory Cost
1	4	$ 840
2	3	600
3	4	820
4	2	380
5	1	240
6	3	570
7	3	580
8	4	770
Totals	24	$4,800

2. Average cost per supervisor
   Supervisor cost = $4,800/24 = $200
3. Supervisory expense for budgetary use

Average of past cost	$200
Expected wage increase	10
Budgeted weekly supervisory cost	$210

Figure 3-2

Monthly Supplies Expense for Assembly
Department

Month	DLH	Expense
January	1,200	$ 170
February	1,350	180
March	1,450	200
April	1,000	160
May	1,200	175
June	1,450	185
July	2,000	260
August	2,150	265
September	1,950	255
October	1,650	230
November	1,400	180
December	1,200	170
Total	18,000	$2,430
Average	1,500	$ 203

Figure 3-3

cuss the level of expenditure for such items as advertising and sales promotion with the marketing executives who decide how much to spend. Past data on expenditures in relation to sales volume may be helpful, but they rarely provide a reliable guide to future spending levels because expense amounts are determined directly by a specific decision.

Semifixed Costs

Historical averages, however, do furnish a useful starting point for measuring semifixed expenses. But before he examines the historical cost information, the accountant must determine the volume ranges over which the costs are expected to remain constant. He can then divide this dollar amount by, for example, the number of supervisors working at that volume, to arrive at a cost per supervisor. This cost per supervisor is next adjusted for future salary increases and for expected changes in work procedures that will affect the number of supervisors used for each volume range. The resulting number can be used for planning and controlling the semifixed expense.

For instance, in Figure 3-2 the number of supervisors for each of eight weeks is accumulated, along with the supervisory cost for each of those weeks. The average of these costs is calculated as $200 per supervisor, and this cost is adjusted for an expected salary increase to arrive at a weekly supervisory cost of $210. Instead of using historical data, this cost estimate could be based on a plant manager's estimate or on an analysis of salary data obtained from the personnel department.

Semivariable Costs

The technique of data analysis is commonly used for separating the fixed portion of the semivariable expense from the variable portion. The most familiar three techniques are: the scattergraph method, the semiaverage method, and the least squares method. Each of these methods is illustrated in the following paragraphs by analyzing the data of Figure 3-3. These data, taken from the accounting records, show the dollar amounts of factory supplies charged to a producing department for each of the preceding 12 months.

When using the scattergraph method to separate the fixed and variable costs included in these data, the accountant plots the numbers on a graph, as in Figure 3-4. The following procedure is used in plotting the information on the graph. First the accountant locates a point directly above the number of direct labor hours (DLH) for a month; next he moves this point upward until it is directly across from the dollar amount for that level of direct labor hours, placing a mark on the graph at that spot. The data for April are identified on the graph in Figure 3-4 by the arrows. The data for each month are similarly plotted; then a line is visually fitted to the data.

The point at which the line crosses the vertical axis measures the amount of the fixed cost, and the slope of the line measures the rate at which the variable cost changes for each unit change in activity. The fixed portion of the expense ($50) is read directly from the graph in Figure 3-4, and the variable rate is computed by subtracting the fixed portion of the expense ($50) from the average expense ($203) to calculate the total variable cost. The total variable cost ($153) is divided by the average direct labor hours (1,500) for the amount ($.102) that the expense changes with each one-hour change in direct labor hours.

The semiaverage method produces similar results without the use of a graph. With the semiaverage method, data are divided into two groups: one group includes that half the data for the periods with high levels of activity, and the other group includes data for the periods with low levels of activity. In Figure 3-5, for example, the information for the 12 months is split into two groups of data, each group containing 6 months of activity.

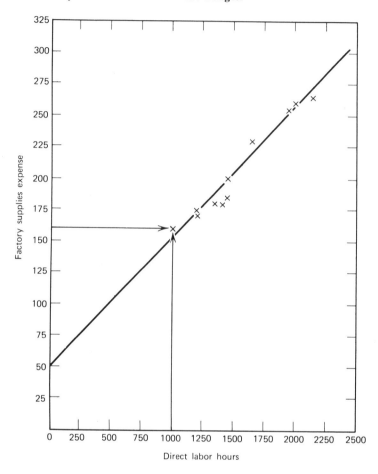

Figure 3-4   Scattergraph analysis of factory supplies expense: fixed amount $50.00; variable rate: ($203 − $50)/1,500 = $.102.

The average direct labor hours and expense are computed for each group of data; next the variable rate of expense per labor hour ($.109) is computed by dividing the expense difference ($60) by the direct labor hour difference (550). This variable rate is applied to the average hours (1,500) for the average total variable cost ($163.50). In turn, this total is deducted from the average total cost ($203) for the fixed amount per month ($39.50).

The third method for separating the fixed and variable costs is the least squares technique, which operates in a manner similar to the scattergraph except the line is fitted to the data by a mathematical formula. The line is fitted to the data in such a manner that the total of the squares of the vertical distances between each data point and the line is at a minimum. Although the mathematical derivation of the formula used for computing the least squares line is a bit messy, the application of the formula to a set of data is relatively simple.

To illustrate this technique, the supplies expense data given in Figure 3–3 are analyzed in Figure 3-6 using the least squares procedure. The first three columns contain the information presented in Figure 3-3, and the four columns on the right contain the calculations required by the least squares technique. In the middle two columns of data, the plus or minus sign is important for the individual values because the sign indicates whether the amount is above (plus) or below (minus) the average. For example, the

Semiaverage Analysis of Factory Supplies Expense for Assembly Department

Six High Months			Six Low Months		
Month	DLH	Expense	Month	DLH	Expense
March	1,450	$ 200	January	1,200	$ 170
June	1,450	185	February	1,350	180
July	2,000	260	April	1,000	160
August	2,150	265	May	1,200	175
September	1,950	255	November	1,400	180
October	1,650	230	December	1,200	170
Total	10,650	$1,395	Total	7,350	$1,035
Average	1,775	$ 233	Average	1,225	$ 173

	Average DLH	Average Expense
High months	1,775	$233
Low months	1,225	173
Difference	550	$ 60

Variable rate: $60/550 = $.109
Fixed amount: $203 − (1,500 × .109) = $39.50

Figure 3-5

Least Squares Analysis of Factory Supplies Expense for Assembly Department

Month	DLH	Expense	Variance from Average DLH (X)	Variance from Average Expense (Y)	XY	X^2
January	1,200	$ 170	−300	−33	9,900	90,000
February	1,350	180	−150	−23	3,450	22,500
March	1,450	200	−50	−3	150	2,500
April	1,000	160	−500	−43	21,500	250,000
May	1,200	175	−300	−28	8,400	90,000
June	1,450	185	−50	−18	900	2,500
July	2,000	260	+500	+57	28,500	250,000
August	2,150	265	+650	+62	40,300	422,500
September	1,950	255	+450	+52	23,400	202,500
October	1,650	230	+150	+27	4,050	22,500
November	1,400	180	−100	−23	2,300	10,000
December	1,200	170	−300	−33	9,900	90,000
Total	18,000	$2,430			152,750	1,455,000
Average	1,500	203				

Variable rate $= \Sigma XY / \Sigma X^2$
Variable rate: 152,750/1,455,000 = $.105
Fixed amount: $203 − (1,500 × .105) = $45.50, or $46

Figure 3-6

1,200 direct labor hours worked in January is 300 hours below the average of 1,500. Likewise, the $170 of supplies expense for January is $33 below the average. Multiplying the hourly deviation from the average (−300) by the dollar deviation from the average (−$33) provides the total dollar deviation for the month ($9,900), shown in the second column from the right. The hourly deviations from the average for each month are then squared, yielding the amounts in the right-hand column. The totals of the two columns on the right are used to compute the variable amount of expense ($.105) for each direct labor hour worked. This amount is multiplied by average direct labor hours (1,500) to develop the average variable expense

($157.50), which is subtracted from the average total expense ($203) to arrive at the fixed expense per month ($45.50).

Just as the averages computed for variable cost and semifixed cost are adjusted for expected future changes, so must the amount computed with the scattergraph, the semiaverage, or the least squares method be adjusted. If factory supplies are expected to increase in price, or if changes in production methods will require a quantity of supplies different from that of the past, the dollar amounts generated by the analysis of historical data must be adjusted.

In Figure 3-7, for example, the results of the least squares analysis are adjusted upward for expected price increases in supplies expense and for a change in production procedure that will cause a greater quantity of supplies to be used than in the past year. These adjustments result in an expected supplies expense of $50 per month, plus $.12 for each labor hour worked. These expense measurements supply information that can be used by managers in making planning and control decisions. To facilitate these decisions, the cost measurements are usually incorporated in a budget or set of standards, and one of the more difficult expense groups to build into a budget is the overhead expense. This expense is reviewed in the next section.

Computing Budget Amounts for Semivariable Costs

1. Basic data from least squares calculation
   Fixed amount: $46
   Variable rate: $ .105
2. Expected changes affecting factory supplies
   Price increase 5%
   Increased usage because of change in production procedures: $2.20/month;
     $.01/DLH.
3. Budget for factory supplies

	Fixed	Variable
Least squares computation	$45.50	$.105
Price increase	2.30	.005
Production method change	2.20	.010
Budget amount	$50.00	$.120

Figure 3-7

FLEXIBLE OVERHEAD BUDGETS

Manufacturing overhead expense is the name normally used for the expense category that includes all production expenses except direct material and direct labor. The overhead expenses usually represent the cost of the activities and facilities that support the primary productive activities of the firm. Thus certain supplies expenses, supervisory salaries and depreciation expenses are considered to be overhead expenses because they are not directly involved in the production of the company's product.

The identification of cost behavior and the measurement of expense amounts are just as important for overhead expenses as they are for direct material and direct labor. The objective of overhead budgets in a direct cost system is to identify the portions of overhead expense that vary with changes in production volume or some other causal factor and the expenses that remain constant throughout a given time period. Both types of overhead expense are important for planning and control decisions. For example, in product pricing decisions during periods of excess capacity, the variable overhead is relevant to the pricing manager, who needs to know the amount by which total company costs will change for various changes in production. The pricing manager must consider the changes in all costs affected by the change in production level, and a division of overhead expenses into fixed and variable components is essential for providing such information. Such a division is also necessary for cost control decisions made by departmental supervisors. The total costs that should have been incurred in a department during the month can be computed only if overhead expenses are divided into their fixed and variable components.

In a direct cost system, overhead expenses receive the same management attention that labor and material receive. These expenses are considered to be controllable as material and labor, and the direct cost system generates the kind of information that enables company managers to effectively plan and control overhead expenses.

An essential tool in the planning and control of overhead expenses is the flexible overhead budget. This budget tool is based on the assumption that overhead expense behavior can be separated into its fixed and variable components. The overhead expenses are analyzed as are other company expenses: behavior patterns are identified, and dollar amounts for each type of expense are computed. The results of this analysis are then accumulated in a rate and amount budget like the one illustrated in Figure 3-8, in which the overhead expenses that are direct to a production department are listed and the dollar amount by which the cost varies with changes in departmental activity are shown. The variable portion of overhead expense is listed in the "Rate" column and the fixed amount of the expense is included in the "Amount" column. The total of the "Rate" column in Figure 3–8 indicates that overhead expense will change $1.70 for a one-hour change in direct labor hours, and the total of the "Amount" column indicates that the fixed amount of expense per month is $1,325.

The variable expenses in the "Rate" column vary with the volume base identified at the top of the budget. In Figure 3–8, for instance, the overhead expenses vary with direct labor hours, but for another department the expenses may vary with some other factor such as machine hours or units of product. This activity base in the rate and amount budget has a purpose different from that of the volume base used in absorption costing systems. The absorption costing system uses the volume base as a means of computing an overhead cost per unit of product produced. The direct cost system uses the volume base as a surrogate for units of overhead, since overhead cannot be measured in pounds, feet, or gallons. This creation of an overhead unit makes it possible for the accountant to develop forecasts of overhead amounts required for different output levels, and it enables him to provide control reports that identify excess overhead costs caused by using too many overhead units and by wasteful use of individual elements of overhead expense.

For example, assume that the assembly department in Figure 3–8 showed for the past month an unfavorable overhead expense variance of $60 and an unfavorable labor variance of 20 hours. The $60 overhead

Hypothetical Corporation Rate and Amount Budget

Department: Assembly   Period: Month
Supervisor: G. Rind   Base: Direct labor hours

Expense	Rate	Amount
Supervision	$–0–	$ 840
Material handling	.88	60
Factory supplies	.12	50
Depreciation	–0–	200
Maintenance	.70	175
	$1.70	$1,325

Figure 3-8

variance was caused by the use of 20 extra units of overhead which cost $34 (20 hours × $1.70), and the remaining variance of $26 was attributable to the use of more than the budgeted amounts of the expenses listed in the rate and amount budget. If the department supervisor is shown the portion of his overhead variance caused by his using too many units of overhead and the portion caused by inefficient use of the individual overhead items, he is better able to control overhead expenses because he can pinpoint the cause of the expense variance.

The dollar amounts in the rate and amount budget illustrated in Figure 3–8 were developed using the cost behavior identification and cost measurement techniques discussed in Chapter 2 and in the first section of this chapter. For example, the supervision cost in the rate and amount budget is taken from the analysis of supervisory costs demonstrated in Figure 3–2, and the factory supplies expense variable rate and fixed amount were computed by adjusting the results of the least squares analysis (Figure 3–6) for price and production method changes (Figure 3–7) to arrive at the budgeted amounts. The material handling expense amounts were calculated in the same manner as the factory supplies expense, although their computation is not illustrated in this chapter.

Service Department Costs

However, the maintenance cost amounts were derived by analyzing the relationship between the level of activity in the Assembly Department and the quantity of maintenance service required by that department. That is, through analysis of the number of maintenance hours required in the past or through the use of engineering studies, the number of maintenance hours necessary for each direct labor hour worked in the assembly department was determined. If the analysis of past experience is used to determine the relationship between activity levels in a producing department and service required from a service department, the least squares technique can be employed to estimate the fixed and variable portions of service needed during each time period.

To illustrate how this works, the number of hours of maintenance used in the assembly department at Hypothetical Corporation during the past year were analyzed. This calculation appears in Figure 3-9. As the illustration shows, computing the relationship between direct labor hours in the assembly department and maintenance hours used in that department utilizes the same procedure followed in Figure 3–6 to separate the fixed and variable portions of supplies expense. The objective in both cases is to determine how much a variable factor (factory supplies, maintenance labor) changes with changes in direct labor hours, and the least squares technique

Least Squares Analysis of Maintenance Labor Hours Used by Assembly Department

			Variance from Average			
Month	DLH	Mainte-nance Hours	DLH (X)	Mainte-nance Hours (Y)	XY	X^2
January	1,200	155	−300	−15	4,500	90,000
February	1,350	178	−150	+8	−1,200	22,500
March	1,450	153	−50	−17	850	2,500
April	1,000	131	−500	−39	19,500	250,000
May	1,200	126	−300	−44	13,200	90,000
June	1,450	152	−50	−18	900	2,500
July	2,000	258	+500	+88	44,000	250,000
August	2,150	214	+650	+44	28,600	422,500
September	1,950	199	+450	+29	13,050	202,500
October	1,650	200	+150	+30	4,500	22,500
November	1,400	146	−100	−24	2,400	10,000
December	1,200	128	−300	−42	12,600	90,000
Total	18,000	2,040			142,900	1,455,000
Average	1,500	170				

Variable hours: $\Sigma XY/\Sigma X^2$
Variable hours: 142,900/1,455,000 = .09821
Fixed hours per month: 170 − (1,500 × .09821) = 22.68

Maintenance Hours for Assembly Department
Budget

Average variable maintenance hours	.09821
Expected increase in hours	.00179
Budgeted variable maintenance hours	.10000
Averaged fixed hours per month	22.68
Expected increase in hours	2.32
Budgeted maintenance hours per month	25.00

Figure 3-9

Hypothetical Corporation Rate and Amount Budget

Department: Maintenance   Period: Month
Supervisor: I. Fixit   Base: Maintenance labor hours

Expense	Rate	Amount
Maintenance labor	$6	$ –0–
Maintenance supplies	1	50
Depreciation	0	150
Supervision	0	900
	$7	$1,100

Figure 3-10

is useful for developing such information. The results of the least squares computation are adjusted for future expected changes in maintenance use to arrive at a budgeted variable rate for maintenance use of one-tenth maintenance labor hour for each direct labor hour worked in the Assembly Department and a fixed quantity of 25 maintenance hours per month.

However, knowing the number of maintenance hours used in the assembly department does not provide the dollar amounts for the departmental rate and amount budget. To produce these amounts, the maintenance labor hours that are used in the assembly department must be applied to the total of the "rate" column for the maintenance department rate and amount budget. In this budget (Figure 3-10), the dollar amounts were computed using the cost behavior identification and cost measurement procedures already discussed.

In a direct cost system, the $1,100 that appears in the "Amount" column of the maintenance department budget remains in the department and is never charged to a producing department or to another service department. Only the variable costs of the maintenance department are charged to the departments using the services of the maintenance department. For instance, the assembly department is charged $7 for each hour of maintenance service it receives; and because the assembly department expects to use one-tenth of an hour of maintenance service for each direct labor hour worked, one-tenth of $7 ($.70) appears in the "Rate" column of the rate and amount budget (Figure 3–8) for this department. The $175 that appears in the "Amount" column represents the 25 hours of maintenance labor that will be used in Assembly each month, multiplied by the $7 variable maintenance cost.

By showing service department and producing department cost interrelationships in this manner, the direct cost system furnishes information about changes in total company costs for changes in activity in any producing department. For example, increasing the use of direct labor hours by 10 in the assembly department will increase total company overhead costs by $17. Since this amount already includes the service department costs that are affected by the volume change, no additional analyses are required to determine how much overhead costs will change in other departments. Planning decisions benefit from this data arrangement because of the speed with which costs can be computed for various changes in activity levels in different departments.

For example, manufacturing costs can be readily forecast for any mix of products if the cost change for changes in activity is identified for each producing department. The routing of the various products through the production departments pinpoints those departments affected by the changes in product mix. The increases in overhead costs and the decreases in overhead costs for all departments affected by the change in product mix provide company managers with information about the net effect on total factory overhead of the change in product mix. This information on changes in overhead costs plus changes in labor and material costs can be used to compute the optimum product mix for various product prices. Chapter 5 provides a more detailed explanation of this use of rate and amount budgets.

Overhead Activity Measures

In choosing a measure for overhead activity, several factors should be considered. First, the overhead base chosen should cause overhead expenses to increase or decrease in the department to which it is related. For instance, in the assembly department analyzed in Figure 3–6, labor hours cause the various overhead items to increase or decrease as labor hour use goes up or down. If locating a factor that directly causes overhead expense to change is very difficult in a specific case, the base chosen should at least move with overhead expenses.

Another consideration that is important for planning and control decisions is the possibility that a single overhead activity measure for a department may not be adequate. For instance, in some departments machine hours may be a good measure for tooling and power costs, and labor hours may provide the best measure for fringe benefits and payroll overhead. In this case, two rate and amount budgets are set up for the department; one for overhead expenses related to machine hours, and another for overhead expenses related to labor hours. Both budgets are utilized for planning and control by using machine hour and labor hour levels to compute expected costs.

A third consideration in selecting the overhead base is the availability of activity measures. That is, the accountant should whenever possible use an existing statistic that the accounting system already collects and processes. By using a measure that is already available, the accountant avoids all the problems inherent in designing, debugging, and implementing a new data collection procedure. One of the advantages of a measure such as labor hours is that the figure is available and reliable. The same is true of machine hours, when the machine activity is monitored for maintenance purposes.

CHAPTER 4

RESPONSIBILITY ACCOUNTING

Just as cost behavior analysis is essential for reliable dollar amounts in a direct cost system, responsibility accounting is essential for effective planning and control with a direct cost system. People throughout the organization make decisions that affect costs and revenues, and responsibility accounting identifies these individuals and reports to them the consequences of their decisions. Thus responsibility accounting is concerned to a large extent with the interface between the data inputs and outputs and the people who provide and use those data.

BASIC CONCEPTS

The term *responsibility accounting* refers to a system of accounting that relates each cost and revenue item both to the individual who makes decisions affecting that item and to the physical object or activity that causes the expense or revenue to occur. For example, the costs incurred in a producing department are identified with the department supervisor who makes decisions affecting the costs, and the costs are identified with the material or labor to which the cost is attributable. Likewise, sales revenue is identified with the salesman who makes the decisions that result in a sale, and the revenue is identified with the product or product line that generates the revenue.

The classification scheme used in the chart of accounts, then, should recognize this two-dimensional relationship of costs and revenues. This relationship is graphically portrayed in Figure 4-1, and it is cast in a matrix format in Figure 4-2. In Figure 4-2, the expenses or revenues affected by a specific decision maker can quickly be located by scanning the row for a particular decision maker. For instance, decision maker B controls activities 2, 4, and 6. Also, by starting with an object or activity, the manager

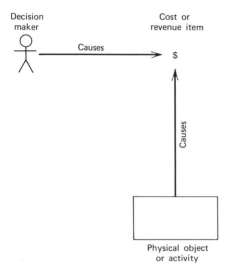

Figure 4-1   The two aspects of responsibility accounting.

(decision maker) who controls the object can be quickly located by scanning the column for the object. Thus the revenues and expenses in a responsibility accounting system are classified by decision maker and by object or activity.

Segment accounting, a concept related to responsibility accounting, requires that for accounting purposes the business be subdivided into small segments, each under the control of one individual. For each segment, in-

Object or activity

Decision maker	1	2	3	4	5	6	7	8	9
A			X		X				
B		X		X		X			
C	X						X		
D								X	X
E		X							

Figure 4-2   Responsibility accounting matrix.

formation about the economic consequences of the decisions made in that segment is reported to the individual in charge of the segment. For accounting purposes, in other words, the manager of a segment is treated as if he were operating an independent business unit, and he is provided with the accounting data needed to manage his segment efficiently.

Two types of accounting segments can be identified: cost segments and revenue generating segments. A cost segment is a segment of the organization in which costs are incurred but no revenue is generated. A production department, for example, incurs costs, but it does not generate revenue directly from the activities performed in the department. The accounting system should provide information to the production department supervisor about the budgeted and actual costs for the department, and the supervisor's performance is evaluated on the basis of how well he controls his costs.

On the other hand, revenue generating departments need information on both costs and revenues. A revenue generating segment is an organization segment that both incurs costs and generates revenues. A sales territory, for example, generates revenue, and it also incurs certain costs. The data in Figure 4-3 illustrate the kind of information the accounting system should furnish to a revenue generating segment. Data on sales revenue, direct

ABC Corporation
Eastern Sales Territory
First Quarter Contribution Forecast

Sales		$250,000
Variable costs		
Production	$80,000	
Marketing	2,000	82,000
Marginal income		168,000
Direct fixed costs		
Salaries	$30,000	
Rent	6,000	
Travel and entertainment	10,000	
Product promotion	12,000	58,000
Territory contribution		$110,000

Figure 4-3   Revenue generating segment data.

variable costs, direct fixed costs, and contribution are supplied to the territory manager. The contribution amount for the territory is the figure that is used to evaluate the performance of the territory manager. No net income figure is computed for a revenue generating segment because such a computation requires the charging of an expense to the territory that is beyond the influence of the territory manager's decisions. Every revenue and expense item listed in the contribution forecast in Figure 4-3 is affected by the territory manager's decisions.

BUSINESS ORGANIZATION AND RESPONSIBILITY ACCOUNTING

Because expenses and revenues must be related to the individual decision maker who controls them, a knowledge of company organization is essential to an effective responsibility accounting system.* Moreover, a company must have an effective organization before responsibility accounting can function properly. The responsibility accounting system cannot make a poorly organized company function effectively; the accounting system will reflect the company organization—sound or unsound. Installing a responsibility accounting system may point out weaknesses in the existing organization, but the accounting system will only make the weaknesses stand out more strongly—it will not eliminate them.

One of the devices most frequently used to describe authority–responsibility relationships in a business is the organization chart. In clearly identifying who is responsible for specific segments of the organization, the chart tells which individuals make decisions that affect the various organization segments. Figure 4-4 illustrates an abbreviated organization chart for a hypothetical logging company. As the chart shows, the president of the company has ultimate responsibility for all company activities. To accomplish the organization objectives, however, the president has subdivided his work by sharing his responsibilities with three vice-presidents. Each of these, in turn, shares his responsibility with several subordinates, and so forth. Consequently, the duties and responsibilities of managers throughout the organization are clearly pictured in the organization chart.

Because business organizations are dynamic, ever-changing enterprises, the organization chart must be frequently updated to reflect the current organization structure. The formal organization chart produced by the com-

---

* See Maurice B. T. Davies, "Organization as a Basis for Control," *The Internal Auditor* (Winter 1963), pp. 40–54, for a concise summary of organization principles.

pany personnel department provides a starting point, but this chart should not be used as the foundation of the responsibility accounting system until it has been compared with the existing organization. Occasionally company politics will dictate that a certain individual occupy a box near the top of the formal organization chart when in fact the individual has no significant duties. In cases like this, the accountant should prepare his own "bootleg" organization chart that accurately reflects the existing organization. This "bootleg" chart is then used in setting up the responsibility accounting system.

Changes in the organization structure are likely to happen more frequently near the upper levels of the organization; thus positions near the

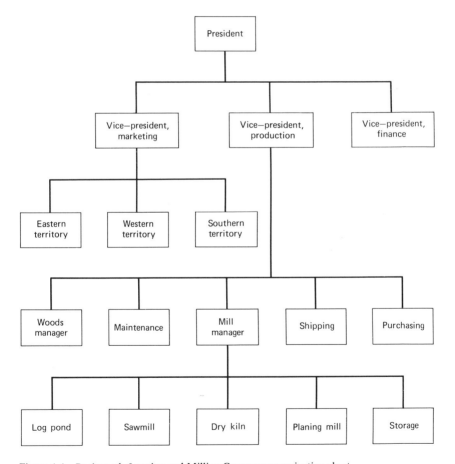

Figure 4-4   Backwoods Logging and Milling Company organization chart.

top managerial levels of the existing organization should be examined first to see whether they conform to the existing company organization chart. Next the middle management positions are compared against the existing organization chart, and so on, until an accurate organization chart is developed.

Two types of responsibility—direct and indirect—are usually associated with responsibility accounting. Direct responsibility includes decisions that directly influence expenses or revenues. For instance, the supervisor of the sawmill in the organization chart in Figure 4-4 has direct responsibility for the labor cost incurred in his department because his decisions have a direct impact on these expenses. Furthermore, the impact of his decisions on the various expenses will be evident shortly after he makes each decision. Also, the supervisor who is directly responsible for an expense is the only person in the organization who has authority to charge an expense to his department. The sawmill supervisor in Figure 4-4, for instance, is the only individual at Backwoods Logging who is authorized to charge expenses to the sawmill department. If the vice-president of production can purchase material for the sawmill department without consulting the sawmill supervisor, the vice-president is directly responsible for the expense, because he makes the decision to incur it. Moreover, this expense should appear on the report for the vice-president and not on the sawmill supervisor's report. In other words, direct responsibility refers to those cases in which a specific expense is charged to the individual who makes the decision that causes the company to incur the expense.

Indirect responsibility, in contrast, is associated with decisions that influence costs or revenues through subordinate behavior. For example, the costs for which the same sawmill supervisor is directly responsible are the indirect responsibility of the mill manager. The latter controls the sawmill costs indirectly through the sawmill supervisor. The manager who is indirectly responsible for a cost or revenue item controls it by hiring the right people and by properly supervising them once they begin to work. He does not control costs for which he is indirectly responsible by trying to "second-guess" his subordinates. A manager may have both direct and indirect responsibility. For an illustration, assume that the vice-president of marketing decides how much to spend on national advertising and the territory managers determine the dollar amount to spend on advertising in their respective territories. In this situation, the vice-president for marketing has direct responsibility for national advertising expenditures and indirect responsibility for territory advertising expense.

Determination of direct and indirect responsibility for costs and revenues has significance for how managers make decisions and for the way in which accounting reports are prepared. Managers who have indirect responsibility for costs and revenues must carefully manage their subordinates to plan and control expenses and revenues. However, managers who have direct responsibility for costs and revenues must plan and control the physical and human resources under their responsibility to perform effectively. Accounting reports are affected by the kind of responsibility an individual has because this factor determines the amount of detail he receives in his report. A manager who is directly responsible for a group of expenses receives a detailed report itemizing each expense incurred. He needs detailed information in his report to permit him to see the impact his decisions have had on his expenses. Then, too, he may also need more frequent reports on those expenses for which he is directly responsible than those for which he is indirectly responsible.

Managers with indirect responsibility for expenses should receive report summaries that pinpoint subordinates who are having problems. In the organization represented in Figure 4-4, for example, the mill manager should receive a report that provides a one-number (or, at the most, a few numbers) summary of the performance of each of the five supervisors reporting to him. His report should include no details about the specific expenses incurred in the departments reporting to him, since his decisions do not directly affect these expenses.

It is also characteristic of responsibility accounting that an expense is never charged to an organization segment unless the supervisor of that segment influences the expense directly with his decisions or indirectly through the decisions of his subordinates. None of the plant manager's expenses are allocated to individual operating departments, and none of the fixed costs of service departments are spread among the departments using the service. If costs are allocated to organization segments that benefit from the costs, the decision maker who receives the cost allocation is charged with an expense that his decisions do not influence. Accordingly, he will either ignore the cost allocated to his department, or he will waste a great deal of his time arguing with the accounting department about the manner in which he is charged with the expense. In either case, no productive activity results.

Even if no arbitrary cost allocations are made, the charges to producing departments for services received from service departments are frequently a source of trouble. The producing department will complain that service department costs are out of line because service department personnel are inefficient. Service department supervisors, in turn, will argue that the producing departments are to blame for the high costs incurred. The variations are infinite, but there is no need for this kind of argument to take place if a sound responsibility accounting system is used.

The problem in this case is that the supervisors of two organization segments both influence the same cost; that is, the supervisors are jointly responsible for the same cost. The supervisor of the maintenance department influences total maintenance cost, and the production departments that use the maintenance services influence total maintenance cost. The same is true of material cost: the purchasing department influences the price paid for the material, and the using departments in the factory influence the quantity of material used. Both organization segments influence the material cost.

In cases such as these, when two segments are influencing the amount of an expense, standard cost techniques can be used to effectively split the responsibility for the cost. Maintenance costs, for example, can be charged to the using department at a standard amount for the work performed. A set of maintenance standards is prepared for maintenance activities, and the standard time for a maintenance activity is charged to the department receiving the service, regardless of the actual time required to perform the job. This approach makes the supervisor of the department in which the maintenance is performed responsible for the quantity of maintenance chores performed in his department, and the maintenance supervisor is responsible for getting the work done within the standard time allowed. The responsibility for material cost is divided in the same way. Material is charged to producing departments at the standard price; thus fluctuations in the material cost charged to a department are caused only by variations in quantity used. Price variances from standard are charged to the purchasing department.

If more than two departments influence a cost, the solution is less simple. One way of handling this situation is to charge the cost to each department that influences it. This approach has a drawback, however, in that each department charged with the cost may have so little influence on the cost that no department feels responsible for the cost. A better solution to this problem is to charge the cost to an individual in the organization who has authority over the several departments that influence the cost.

However, the accounting system should not be expected to reflect all the complex relationships existing in the organization, nor should the accounting system be expected to reflect "fairly" the results of every transaction recorded in the system. Responsibility accounting presumes that company managers are reasonably intelligent decision makers who recognize that the accounting system reports only a selected portion of the total information available within the organization. For example, unfavorable material usage variances in a production department may be caused by poor quality materials purchased because of a material supply shortage, yet the unfavorable material variance will appear in the production department report. In this case, company managers should recognize that the variance is not caused by the department manager on whose report the variance appears. Nevertheless, even though the accounting system does provide a simplified picture of organization complexities, companies receive a great deal of practical benefit from assigning responsibility for costs and revenues, even though the assignment is not perfect.

RESPONSIBILITY REPORTING SYSTEMS

Although responsibility accounting systems provide information for both planning and control, the control function of responsibility accounting has received a great deal of attention in the accounting literature.* This aspect of responsibility accounting relates to the report structure that is used in a responsibility accounting system; and the next few pages are devoted to a discussion of responsibility reporting systems.

One of the essential ingredients of the responsibility reporting system is an organization chart that identifies segment responsibilities. The organiza-

Backwoods Logging and Milling Company

Department: Sawmill   Period: April
Supervisor: J. Igsaw

Expense	Budget	(Over) or Under Budget
Supervision and clerical	$ 1,200	$ (160)
Labor		
Head rig	22,000	60
Resaw	15,000	(370)
Gangsaw	4,000	1,070
Edger	6,000	600
Trimmer	13,000	(3,000)
Stacker	6,000	(60)
Pallets	6,000	(140)
	$73,200	$(2,000)

Figure 4-5   Departmental responsibility report.

* See References at end of chapter for selections for further reading on this subject.

Department: Mill Manager   Period: April
Supervisor: S. Plane

Expense	Budget	(Over) or Under Budget
Mill manager's office		
Supervision	$ 1,200	$ (40)
Clerical	600	50
Total	$ 1,800	$ 10
Subordinate departments		
Log pond	$ 7,000	$ 400
Sawmill[a]	73,200	(2,000)
Dry kiln	25,000	(600)
Planing mill	80,000	1,500
Storage	30,000	(200)
	$217,000	$ (890)

[a] Amounts carried forward from lower level report in Figure 4–5.

Figure 4-6   Summary responsibility report.

tion chart in Figure 4-4 serves as the framework for which a set of responsibility reports are developed in the following examples.

The bottom level of reports in the production function for Backwoods Logging and Milling Company include the five departments reporting to the mill manager. Each of the department supervisors receives a report similar to the report for the sawmill department (see Figure 4-5). To simplify the illustration; only one departmental report is given at this point. Note that this report includes detailed information about each of the expenses incurred in the department, since the department supervisor is directly responsible for these expenses. Also, the department supervisor's name appears on the report, to emphasize that these costs are his responsibility.

The manager to whom the sawmill supervisor reports also receives a summary of monthly activities for each of the departments reporting to him. His report, illustrated in Figure 4-6, includes a section for the expenses for which the mill manager is directly responsible. The total budgeted expenses of $73,200 and the total budget variances of ($2,000) are carried upward from the sawmill supervisor's report to the mill manager's report. The budget amounts and variances for the other departments are assembled in the same manner. This report allows the mill manager to see at a glance which subordinate is having trouble and which ones are operating within the budget. If the mill manager wants detailed information about the individual expenses incurred in any of the departments reporting to him, he can call in the supervisor of the department and review the departmental report with him.

The production vice-president receives a report (Figure 4-7) that summarizes the budget performance of all individuals reporting to him. As in the mill manager's report, expenses are separated into those for which the vice-president has direct responsibility and those for which he has indirect responsibility. Also, the totals for the departments reporting to him have been carried forward from the individual departmental reports. For example, the total budgeted expense for the mill manager for $217,000 and

Backwoods Logging and Milling Company

Department: Vice-President of Production
Supervisor: I. Produce   Period: April

Expense	Budget	(Over) or Under Budget
Vice-president's office	$ 4,000	$ (200)
Subordinate departments		
Woods manager	180,000	(5,000)
Maintenance	6,000	(800)
Mill manager[a]	217,000	(890)
Shipping	22,000	(1,600)
Purchasing	4,000	200
	$433,000	$(8,290)

[a] Amounts carried forward from lower level report in Figure 4-6.

Figure 4-7   Production vice-president responsibility report.

Backwoods Logging and Milling Company

Department: Vice-President of Marketing
Supervisor: W. Sellit   Period: April

Item	Budget	Budget Variance
Expense		
Vice-president's office	$ 8,000	$ (600)
Subordinate departments		
Eastern territory	2,000	60
Western territory	3,000	200
Southern territory	2,500	(500)
Total expenses	$ 15,500	$ (840)
Revenue		
Eastern territory	$100,000	$ 2,000
Western territory	250,000	(1,500)
Southern territory	150,000	(1,000)
Total revenue	$500,000	$ (500)

Figure 4-8   Marketing vice-president responsibility report.

the total budget variances of ($890) are taken from the report for the mill manager in Figure 4-6.

The techniques yielding responsibility reports that pyramid from the lowest producing department to the office of the production vice-president can also be used to generate responsibility reports for marketing. A summary report for the marketing vice-president (Figure 4-8) shows the expense and revenue performance for each sales territory reporting to the marketing vice-president. Contribution reports by territory are not used at this point because they are covered in detail in Chapter 7. However, the idea that market reports for revenue generating segments can be summarized by responsibility areas is clearly illustrated in Figure 4-8. This report enables the marketing vice-president to easily evaluate the cost and revenue performance of each of his territories.

The statement for the president of the company is the final link in the chain of responsibility reports. This report presents a concise picture of the total company activities for April. Deviations from the budget plan are identified by responsibility segment, telling the president which vice-president to call for an explanation of why targeted net income was not attained in April. The vice-president, in turn, can review his report to see which subordinate is responsible for deviations from plan, and so forth, until the bottom departmental level is reached. This identification of deviations from the budget plan is possible because the reports follow directly the organization chart illustrated in Figure 4-4. A comparison of the mill manager's report (Figure 4-6) with the organization chart (Figure 4-4) indicates that expenses for April for each of the departments responsible to the mill manager are summarized in his report. The same relationship holds true for the vice-president of production (Figure 4-7), the vice-president of marketing (Figure 4-8), and the president (Figure 4-9).

Backwoods Logging and Milling Company

Department: President   Period: April
Supervisor: J. Smith

Organization Segment		Budget Variance[a]
Vice-President of marketing[b] (Figure 4-8)		
Revenue	$500,000	$ (500)
Expense	$ 15,500	$ (840)
Vice-president of production[b] (Figure 4-7)	433,000	(8,290)
Vice-president of finance	10,000	(400)
Total budgeted expenses	$458,500	$(10,030)
Total budget variances	(10,030)	
Actual expenses	$468,530	
Actual net income before taxes	$ 31,470	

[a] Reduction in budgeted net income before taxes shown in parentheses.
[b] Amounts carried forward from lower level report.

Figure 4-9   Presidential responsibility report.

The development of the budget amounts in the reports, the problems of charging costs from service departments to producing departments, and the development of contribution reports were not discussed in this chapter, to allow the reader to focus his attention on the cumulative buildup of reports from the lowest levels of the organization to the very top level. However, the techniques and problems involved in production reporting systems are examined at length in Chapter 6, and the contribution reports for revenue generating segments are illustrated in detail in Chapter 7.

REFERENCES

Control Function of Responsibility Accounting

1. Higgins, John A. "Responsibility Accounting," *The Arthur Andersen Chronicle*, (April 1952). This is one of the original articles on the subject, and it contains a detailed example of responsibility reports.
2. Hindman, W. R., "Responsibility Budgeting," *Managerial Planning* (formerly *Managerial Budgeting*) (May 1965), pp. 12–15. This article provides a good summary of how responsibility budgeting should be used.
3. Krueger, Donald A., "Responsibility Accounting ... in Perspective," *The Arthur Andersen Chronicle*, (December 1966), pp. 27–37.
4. Netten E. W., "Responsibility Accounting for Better Management," *The Canadian Chartered Accountant*, (September 1963), pp. 164–168.

General

5. Davies, Maurice B. T., "Organization As a Basis for Control," *The Internal Auditor* (Winter 1963), pp. 40–54.

CHAPTER 5

DIRECT PRODUCT COSTS

For cost control, identification of costs with decision makers is essential; but for profit planning, identification of costs with products and product lines is critical. Accordingly, this chapter is devoted to a discussion of product cost development for companies using a direct cost system. The problems of compiling costs for discrete and joint products are examined, and the development of a standard product cost for units of product is illustrated.

DISCRETE PRODUCT COSTS

Discrete products are those products for which the production process functions in a manner that allows the product output for one product to vary without affecting directly the production of another product. For example, a company producing television sets can vary the production output of its portable sets without changing its output of cabinet model sets. Of course, if production facilities are operating at capacity, changes in output of one product will affect the output of others, but this change is caused by the limited production capacity, not by the production process itself. This situation can be contrasted with the case of joint product manufacture, in which changes in the output of one product do affect the output of other products.

Assembling Product Costs

Product costs in a direct cost system are generated from the same data that are used for planning and controlling production segment activities. Consequently, organizations that have a well-defined departmental structure in their production function need only analyze the cost behavior in these de-

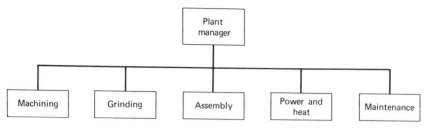

Figure 5-1   Hypothetical Corporation factory organization chart.

partments to arrive at the departmental costs required for computing product costs. The production plant organization chart illustrated in Figure 5-1 identifies the responsibility areas within the plant to which costs are charged. The flow of costs through these departments is represented in Figure 5-2.

Costs are initially charged either to a service department or to a producing department. The variable portion of the service department cost

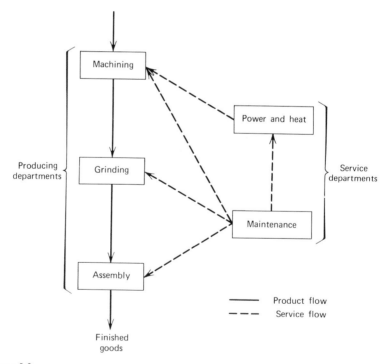

Figure 5-2

flows to a producing department or to another service department, but eventually it arrives at a producing department, where it becomes part of that department's overhead cost. The variable portion of the production department costs is then attached to the units of product that flow through each production department. These variable costs include variable overhead expenses, and therefore the part of the service department cost that is variable to a producing department becomes part of the product cost. All departmental fixed costs remain either in a service department or in a production department. None of the fixed costs are attached to the unit of product as it passes through the plant. For discrete products, the product cost objective is the development of a unit cost that approximates the increase in total company costs for a one-unit increase in output. Attaching any amount of fixed cost to the product would prevent the system from attaining this objective.

Moreover, if a company uses a standard cost system, the standard direct cost of a unit of product will closely approximate the increase in total company costs for a one-unit change in output. This is because the labor, material, and overhead costs included in the standard unit costs reflect the expected cost levels for the future planning period. Historical averages for labor and material may be helpful in estimating future costs, but the product cost used for planning purposes must reflect expected future prices and operating conditions. Standard product costs are ideal for planning decisions because they are based on expected future prices and operating efficiencies. Because of the importance of using expected future costs in planning decisions, all numerical examples in this chapter presume that a standard cost system is in use.

A numerical example of cost flow through the departments mentioned in Figure 5-2 is provided in Figure 5-3. In this example, the manufacturing process begins in the machining department, where material with a cost of $8 is put into process. Two hours of labor is added at a cost of $10, and overhead cost of $4 is added. The overhead cost includes variable costs from both the power and heat department and the maintenance department. The machining department variable overhead rate of $.50 includes a portion of the maintenance cost that is charged directly to the machining department, plus a portion of the maintenance cost that is charged directly to the power and heat department. The maintenance cost that is charged to the power and heat department becomes part of the variable overhead rate of $.50 in that department, and this amount is used to compute the charging rate for power used in the machining department. The rate for power that is charged to the machining department is included in the $.50 variable overhead rate for this department, and this rate ($.50) is

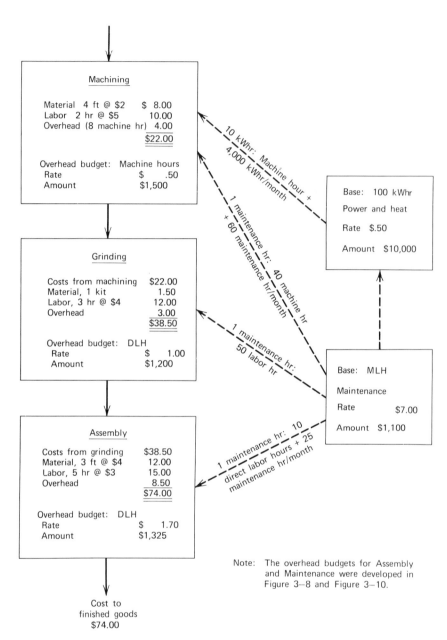

Machining

Material	4 ft @ $2	$ 8.00
Labor	2 hr @ $5	10.00
Overhead	(8 machine hr)	4.00
		$22.00

Overhead budget:	Machine hours
Rate	$ .50
Amount	$1,500

10 kWhr: Machine hour +
4,000 kWhr/month

1 maintenance hr:
+ 60 maintenance hr/month

1 maintenance hr: 40 machine hr

Base:	100 kWhr
Power and heat	
Rate	$.50
Amount	$10,000

Grinding

Costs from machining	$22.00
Material, 1 kit	1.50
Labor, 3 hr @ $4	12.00
Overhead	3.00
	$38.50

Overhead budget:	DLH
Rate	$ 1.00
Amount	$1,200

1 maintenance hr:
50 labor hr

Base:	MLH
Maintenance	
Rate	$7.00
Amount	$1,100

Assembly

Costs from grinding	$38.50
Material, 3 ft @ $4	12.00
Labor, 5 hr @ $3	15.00
Overhead	8.50
	$74.00

Overhead budget:	DLH
Rate	$ 1.70
Amount	$1,325

1 maintenance hr: 10
direct labor hours + 25
maintenance hr/month

Note: The overhead budgets for Assembly and Maintenance were developed in Figure 3–8 and Figure 3–10.

Cost to
finished goods
$74.00

Figure 5-3

used to compute the overhead cost that goes into the unit of product. This is how a portion of the variable service department cost eventually becomes part of the product cost.

After work has been completed on the product in the machining department, all the costs directly caused by the production of that unit of product ($22) are moved to the grinding department, where additional costs are incurred. When the product moves from Machining to Grinding, appropriate accounting entries are made to remove the cost from Machining and to add it to Grinding. In the grinding department additional material, labor, and overhead costs amounting to $16.50 are added, and a total of $38.50 is transferred to the assembly department. This department completes the product by adding costs of $35.50, and the total, ($74) is then transferred to finished goods inventory. From here the costs are moved to the various revenue generating segments and are eventually consolidated in a company income statement. The total plant fixed costs of $15,125 are also eventually consolidated into the company income statement as a period charge. That is, these costs are considered to be the monthly cost of providing productive capacity that permits the manufacture of units of product.

Although no fixed costs can be traced to the individual units of product manufactured in the plant in this example, it is possible for fixed costs to be directly traceable to a product; however, the traceability is to the total output for a time period. None of the fixed costs is traceable to individual units of product. This situation can arise when a department or an entire plant is devoted to the production of a single product. In Figure 5-3, for example, only one product is considered. If this is the only product produced in the plant, the total monthly plant fixed costs of $15,125 are a direct fixed cost of the product fabricated in that plant. Or, if the machining department worked on only one product, the $1,500 of fixed cost for that department would be a direct fixed cost of the product. These direct fixed costs are used in decisions that evaluate the adequacy of planned or actual product contribution or product line contribution.

Using Product Costs for Planning

Although historical unit costs are useless for cost control decisions, standard product costs are helpful in arriving at various planning decisions. Pricing decisions, for instance, benefit from standard unit cost information. The standard direct unit cost provides a floor below which a company is unwilling to lower its unit price if it wants to avoid selling at a price that is lower than the incremental cost of producing the product.

Apex Corporation
Forecast Contribution by Products
July 19XX

	Company	Able	Baker
Net sales	$60,000	$35,000	$25,000
Variable costs			
Production	26,000	16,000	10,000
Marketing	6,000	3,500	2,500
Total	32,000	19,500	12,500
Marginal income	28,000	15,500	12,500
Direct fixed costs			
Marketing	5,000	4,000	1,000
Production	7,500	2,000	5,500
Total	12,500	6,000	6,500
Product contribution	15,500	$ 9,500	$ 6,000
Common fixed costs			
Marketing	2,000		
Production	2,500		
Administration	6,000		
Total common	10,500		
Net income before taxes	$ 5,000		

Figure 5-4

Also, the standard direct product cost information is useful in developing contribution targets for revenue generating segments and for evaluating the adequacy of product contribution. In Figure 5-4, for example, the standard direct unit cost information is used to develop a schedule that identifies the contribution generated by each product. This schedule arranges the information in a manner that allows managers to readily evaluate the effect on product contribution of selling price changes, changes in direct marketing costs, or changes in sales volume. The impact on product contribution of these various changes is made possible by the standard direct unit product cost, which shows the changes in production costs for various levels of activity in the marketing function. A much more detailed discussion of the use of direct product costs for planning is presented in Chapters 8 and 9, but for now this brief discussion can serve as an introduction to the use of direct product cost information for planning decisions.

JOINT PRODUCT COSTS

Joint products are produced simultaneously by a production process; the mix of products may be varied, but varying the output of one product will usually cause output of other products to vary in the same manner. For instance, a meat packer does not slaughter a round steak, he must slaughter a steer, which provides steaks, hides, and trimmings. Increasing the output of round steaks increases the production of hides and trimmings, and vice versa.

Developing Joint Product Costs

The problem in arriving at direct joint product costs is that large groups of expenses are variable costs, but they vary with the output of a group of products instead of with the output of a single product. Consequently, these expenses are not direct costs of individual products but of groups of products, and they cannot be assigned to specific products. The cost flows for this type of production process are illustrated in Figure 5-5. Here the product is put into production in department A, from which two separate product streams flow. One of the streams moves to department B and the other to department C, but none of the direct variable costs incurred in department A are transferred to either of the two receiving departments. This is because the two streams of product are produced jointly by the process in department A, and none of department A's cost is traceable to either product stream. However, the direct variable costs of department A are not ignored; they are carried to the end of the group of departments as a direct variable cost of the total group of products produced by these departments.

The same is true for the direct variable costs incurred in department B, which also has a process that simultaneously produces two streams of product. The direct variable costs of department B are carried to the combined output of departments D and E, since the direct variable costs of

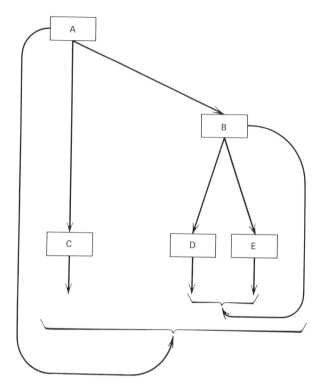

Figure 5-5

department B are traceable to the combined output of these two departments. The only costs that are directly traceable to the individual units of product are those incurred in the last three departments of the production process.

Since direct product costs include only the costs directly traceable to the unit of product, it would seem that the costs incurred in department A and department B should be ignored. However, this is not the case. In developing a direct cost per unit for discrete products, the objective of the direct cost system designer is the development of a unit product cost that approximates the increase in total company cost for a one-unit increase in production. The direct product costs for specific units in a joint production process do not provide this information because there are variable costs that change with output changes but are not traceable to individual units of product. As a result, the direct costs of the total product mix are the relevant costs for planning in a joint production process.

Cost Information for Planning Decisions

As the range of variability of the product mix increases, the importance of identifying direct costs with departments and cost centers also increases. Such identification is essential because the total cost of producing various product mixes from a given input is needed for sound profit planning decisions. When costs are identified with departments and cost behavior patterns are clearly identified, total cost for any mix of products can be easily computed by summing the total cost projected for each of the departments. Figure 5-6 contains departmental direct costs for the joint product flow illustrated in Figure 5-5.

As shown in Figure 5-6, processing 100 gallons of product in department A increases company costs by $9.15, but none of this cost is passed on to department B or department C. The direct cost of processing 100 gallons of product in department B is $2.05, and none of this cost is passed on to department D or department E. The only direct cost that is traceable to the final unit or product is the cost incurred in the last department that processes the product. Thus for 100-gallon lots product X has a direct cost of $6.15, product Y a cost of $9.80, and product Z a cost of $8.25. For planning decisions, however, these costs provide only part of the information needed; the costs of department A and department B must also be included in product planning decisions. For example, the total increase in company costs for processing 10,000 gallons of product with the product mix described in case I in Figure 5-7 is $1,768.50. This figure includes the direct variable costs of all the departments affected by the production of the 10,000 gallons of product. The direct variable costs of each department also furnish information that can be used to evaluate the cost impact of various product mixes.

Case II in Figure 5-7 shows how the direct variable costs of departments D and E are used to evaluate the change in cost caused by altering the mix of joint products flowing from department B. In this case 1,000 gallons is shifted from the stream of product that flows to department E and is added to the stream of product that flows to department D. As a result of this change in product mix, total company costs increase by $15.50. Various other product mixes can be evaluated in the same manner to determine the cost effect of different combinations of product output. When selling prices are combined with the cost analysis, the product mix that generates the maximum marginal income can be readily calculated. This form of analysis is illustrated in Chapter 8, along with other forms of contribution and marginal income analysis.

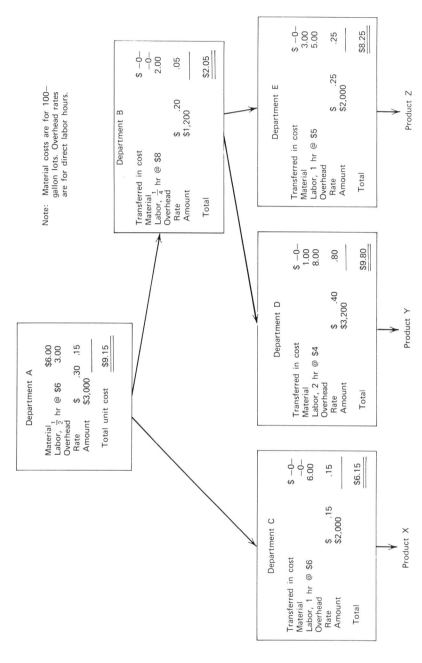

Figure 5-6

Case I
Product flow
Department A processes 10,000 gallons of material, resulting in 5,000 gallons of each of the two products produced jointly in department A. One stream of product moves to department C, where it is processed into 5,000 gallons of product X. The other product stream moves to department B, where it is converted into two streams of product that are produced jointly. From department B, 2,000 gallons of product moves to department D, and the remaining 3,000 gallons goes to department E.
Costs for planning

Department A (100 × $9.15)	$	915.00
Department B (50 × 2.05)		102.50
Department C (50 × 6.15)		307.50
Department D (20 × 9.80)		196.00
Department E (30 × 8.25)		247.50
Total	$1	,768.50

Case II
Product flow
The product flow is the same as case I except that department B now sends 3,000 gallons to department D and 2,000 gallons to department E. That is, 1,000 gallons of product is shifted from department E to department D.
Costs for planning

Costs from case I	$1,768.50
Increase in department D costs (10 × $9.80)	98.00
Decrease in department E costs (10 × 8.25)	(82.50)
Total cost for new product mix	$1,784.00
Case II costs	$1,784.00
Case I costs	1,768.50
Cost increase	
[($9.80 − $8.25) × 10]	$ 15.50

Figure 5-7

Unit: One Piece
Product: Spare Part

	Unit Price	Machining	Grinding	Assembly	Total
Material					
4 ft	$2.00	$ 8.00			
1 kit	1.50		$ 1.50		
3 ft	4.00			$12.00	
Total		8.00	1.50	12.00	$21.50
Labor					
Machining, 2 hr	5.00	10.00			
Grinding, 3 hr	4.00		12.00		
Assembly, 5 hr.	3.00			15.00	
Total		10.00	12.00	15.00	$37.00
Overhead					
Machining, 8 machine hr	.50	4.00			
Grinding, 3 labor hr	1.00		3.00		
Assembly, 5 labor hr	1.70			8.50	
Total		4.00	3.00	8.50	$15.50
Total cost		$22.00	$16.50	$35.50	$74.00

Figure 5-8   Product cost card.

PRODUCT COST CARDS

Discrete Products

Product cost cards are used to summarize the standard direct cost information for a particular product. In Figure 5-8, for example, the product cost card summarizes the data presented in Figure 5-3. This cost card identifies costs by object of expenditure (material, labor, overhead) and responsibility area. The total material cost of the product in Figure 5-8 amounts to $21.50, and this amount can be traced to the individual departments in which the cost is incurred. Labor and overhead totals can be similarly traced to the departments in which the cost is incurred.

Product cost cards enable a company to quickly update its standard product cost as material, labor, or overhead costs change. Only the cost element that has changed is altered on the product cost card, and a new standard product cost is quickly computed. The cost that is transferred from a department with the completed product can be read from the product cost card by referring to the total direct cost incurred in a department. For instance, the $22 of cost that was transferred from the machining department in Figure 5-3 is the total of the machining department column in Figure 5-8.

Joint Products

Product cost cards take on a different form for joint products because of the production interrelationships among the joint products. Instead of developing a standard cost card for individual units of product, a standard cost card is prepared for the batch of material that produces the group of products. The cost card includes all direct costs incurred from the point at which the material is put into process to the completion of the final products. Figure 5-9 illustrates the form of such a cost card for joint products being produced in a fixed relationship (i.e., the mix of the final products cannot be varied). In Figure 5-9, the refinery producing the gasoline and kerosene always produces the two products in the proportions shown in the example. As the illustration indicates, none of the joint costs are allocated to the final product; these costs are treated as a common cost of producing gasoline and kerosene.

When the product mix is variable, the standard cost card shows the cost formula that is used to compute the cost of any mix of final products. For instance, the data in Figure 5-6 showing the cost change for changes in production activity in the various departments would appear on the cost card. In addition to this cost information, data on the physical constraints that limit the product mix variations would be listed on the card. These data on costs and physical constraints can be used to compute the increase in total company cost for any planned mix of products.

ACTUAL DIRECT PRODUCT COSTS

In all the examples discussed up to this point, a standard cost system was used to demonstrate the accumulation of product cost. This was done to simplify the illustrations and to clearly point out the usefulness of direct product cost information for planning decisions. Actual direct product cost

Unit: Gallon
Products:
1. Gasoline
2. Kerosene

Standard batch size: 100,000 gallons of crude oil

Joint costs			
Refining department costs			
Material	$10,000		
Labor	2,000		
Overhead	4,000		
Total joint costs			$16,000
Direct costs of end products			
Gasoline-treating department costs (40,000 gallons)			
Material	$ 600		
Labor	1,400		
Overhead	1,000		
Total		$3,000	
Kerosene-treating department costs (60,000 gallons)			
Material	$ 400		
Labor	600		
Overhead	1,000		
Total		2,000	
Total direct cost of end products			5,000
Total cost of batch			$21,000

Figure 5-9   Product cost card.

information can be used for planning decisions, but the actual costs reflect past operating conditions and prices. They need to be adjusted for expected future conditions before they are used as inputs to planning decisions.

The product cost flow through the production department is essentially the same for actual costs as for standard costs. The only difference lies in the computation of the cost transferred from a producing department with the completed product. With a standard cost system, only the standard cost of the completed product moves from the department; in an actual cost system, on the other hand, total actual variable cost—which includes cost variances—is transferred to the next department. In an actual cost system, consequently, material waste and labor inefficiency are reflected in the product cost instead of in cost variances. Overhead cost is charged to completed product by using the departmental rate and amount budget to compute the variable overhead cost of the product transferred.

The charges from service departments to other departments are based on the variable costs incurred in the service departments. For instance, the maintenance department bases its charges on the variable cost of providing an hour of maintenance service, and the total variable cost for the actual maintenance hours worked in a department is charged to that department.

In summary, actual variable costs flow from service departments to the producing departments in which they are attached to the units of product. The total actual variable cost incurred in a producing department is moved to succeeding departments with the units of product transferred from the producing department. Eventually all actual variable costs of production are transferred to inventory and from there to the income statement.

CHAPTER 6

PRODUCTION COST REPORTING SYSTEMS

Provision of relevant information for cost control is one of the advantages of a direct cost system, and this chapter presents a review of the type of information that can be generated by a direct cost production reporting system. Since production cost reports serve primarily as cost control tools, let us begin with an overview of the concepts underlying the control process.

CONTROL SYSTEMS

Certain characteristics are present in all control systems; both the system designed to control the flight of an airplane and the system designed to control the level of costs in a production department utilize the same type of information. To control either flight path or production cost, a decision maker must know where he is, or what costs he has incurred; he must know where he should be, or what his cost level should be; and he must be able to correct his flight path or production process to bring the actual results in agreement with the desired end.

For the decision maker to determine his current status, output of the process he controls must be measured, and a feedback loop must be established to report the measurements to the decision maker who controls the process. Output measurement involves selecting a unit of measure and applying it to the output of a process. For production reporting purposes, the data on output measurement of the cost control system are composed of information on the number of units produced in a production department, together with the dollar amount of actual cost incurred in generating that production. This information is important because there is no way for the decision maker to tell whether production or costs are out of control until the actual level of these factors is known.

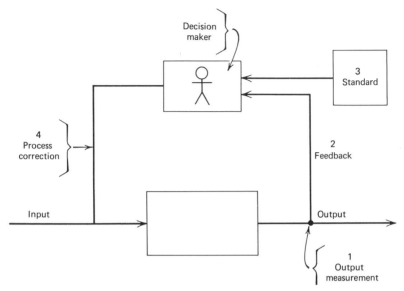

Figure 6-1   Four elements of the control process.

Feedback refers to the procedure whereby the actual costs incurred are reported to a decision maker who has the power to act on what is reported to him. When the actual output is reported to the decision maker, he refers to a standard that tells him what the cost of production should be. This standard may be part of the accounting system or part of the production control system; or, the standard may be stored in the mind of the decision maker. In a standard cost system the standard cost is the standard; in other cases a budgeted amount may serve as the standard. A department supervisor may even use past performance as a standard against which to compare current results. This is a poor form of standard for cost control, but it may be employed by company managers if no budget or standard cost system is in use.

Correcting the process is the final, and most critical, link in the control system. This procedure requires the decision maker who compares the actual output measurement with the standard to take action to bring the two measurements together. For example, if production output is below standard, the production supervisor takes action designed to bring production up to standard. If costs are above standard, the decision maker takes action to bring costs down to standard. In other words, the decision maker moves to change actual output whenever the feedback mechanism indicates a significant difference between actual output and the standard. These four elements of the control process are pictured in Figure 6-1.

Although this relatively simple and mechanistic description of the control process cannot be applied literally to the preparation of production performance reports, it does provide some valuable insights into the function of production performance reports. Consider what the decision maker in Figure 6-1 will do if the standard costs for his department are lowered arbitrarily from a realistic level to an impossible one. According to the preceding discussion, the decision maker will attempt to modify the process to reduce expenses to the standard. However, the new standard is impossible to achieve; thus in spite of his efforts to reduce costs, the decision maker will keep getting messages that indicate costs are out of control. Eventually he will become discouraged and will ignore the feedback messages that indicate costs are out of control. Stated another way, costs cannot be reduced by lowering the budget amount for the costs, and attempts to reduce costs in this manner will probably result in no cost reduction or possibly will even cause costs to increase. This aspect of cost reports is explored more fully in Chapter 13, where the motivational impact of reports is discussed.

The impact on operations of an arbitrary reduction in the standard also helps to point out the difference between cost reduction and cost control. Cost control is the process of maintaining agreement between actual costs and the standard cost (or budgeted cost). In contrast, cost reduction changes the physical characteristics of the department in which the cost is incurred to make the department function more efficiently. For example, new machines may be installed in a department to reduce scrap; employees may be more intensively trained to reduce spoiled units. Such changes in physical operating conditions that improve departmental efficiency are then reflected in a lower cost standard for the department. In short, the cost standard can be reduced by improving the efficiency of the process to be controlled, but the efficiency of the process cannot be improved by merely lowering the standard.

Installation of a direct cost system with complete responsibility accounting can help a company reduce its expenses by identifying the responsibility segments in which there are cost problems. However, it is the alteration of the process causing the cost problem that brings about the reduction in cost, not some arbitrary percentage reduction in the budget standard.

PRODUCTION PERFORMANCE REPORTS

Standard Cost System

With the discussion of the control process as a background, we now begin to examine the kinds of production reports that can be prepared with a direct cost system. First the preparation of performance reports for a standard cost system is illustrated, and then a set of production reports for a company using actual costs is illustrated. The standard cost reports are based on the organization chart and standards data from the discrete product cost discussion in the preceding chapter (Figures 5-1 and 5-3). The organization chart and the standards data are reproduced in Figure 6-2 and 6-3, respectively. The overhead budget for the assembly department is the rate and amount budget that was illustrated in Figure 3-8, and the maintenance department budget comes from Figure 3–10. These data on standards are used to compute the budget amounts in the performance reports illustrated later in this chapter. The same cost standards were used in Chapter 5 to arrive at a standard unit product cost, and the standards are used again in this chapter to provide cost control information; that is to say, the same set of standards furnish information for both product costing and cost control. There is no need for a company to have one standard cost system for generating product costs and another for producing cost control information. Under direct costing one set of standards serves both purposes.

To illustrate the kinds of production performance reports possible with a direct cost system, a production report is prepared for each level of the organization chart (Figure 6-2). Also, a report is developed for the maintenance department to point out the differences between the reports required for producing departments and those used in service departments. The data for actual costs incurred and actual work generated by the various

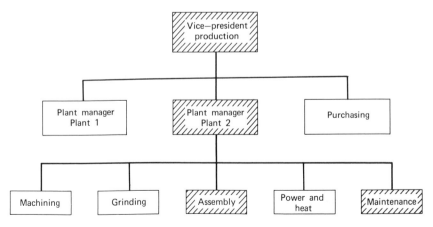

Figure 6-2   Hypothetical Corporation production function organization chart. (Performance reports are illustrated for the shaded boxes.)

Department			Quantity	Unit Cost	Standard Cost per Unit of Output
Machining					
Material			4 ft	$ 2.00	$ 8.00
Labor			2 hr	5.00	10.00
Overhead					
Rate	$	.50	8 machine hr	.50	4.00
Amount	1,500.00				
Grinding					
Cost from Machining			1 unit	22.00	22.00
Material			1 kit	1.50	1.50
Labor			3 hr	4.00	12.00
Overhead					
Rate	$	1.00	3 hr	1.00	3.00
Amount	1,200.00				
Assembly					
Cost from Grinding			1 unit	38.50	38.50
Material			3 ft	4.00	12.00
Labor			5 hr	3.00	15.00
Overhead budget (see Figure 3-8)					

Base: Direct Labor Hours
Period: Month

Expense	Rate	Amount
Supervision	$-0-	$ 840
Material handling	.88	60
Factory supplies	.12	50
Depreciation	-0-	200
Maintenance	.70	175
	$1.70	$1,325

5 hours		8.50

Power and heat
Rate/100 kWh $ .50
Amount $10,000.00

Maintenance
Overhead budget(see Figure 3-10)

Period: Month
Base: Maintenance Labor Hours

Expense	Rate	Amount
Maintenance labor	$6	$ 0
Maintenance supplies	1	50
Depreciation	0	150
Supervision	0	900
	$7	$1,100

Figure 6-3

departments appear in Figure 6-4. These data supply the information on actual output required for the control process such as the one diagrammed in Figure 6-1, and the standards data in Figure 6-3 provide the necessary information on standards. The accountant's job is to combine these two pieces of information in one report which allows the responsible decision maker to see whether the difference between standard and actual is large enough to require action on his part.

To develop this report, the accountant must compute the standard (or budget) cost amount that appears in the report. This amount is developed by calculating the standard cost level for the actual work generated. For instance, the assembly department turned out 1,000 units of product; and because the standard material for each unit produced is $12, the budgeted material in the performance report (Figure 6-5) for the assembly department is $12,000. The $1,000 variance from this standard amount occurred because the assembly department used more than the standard quantity of material. The variance is not due to a price variance, because all material price variances appear in the purchasing department report. In this way the joint responsibility for material cost is separated, with price responsibility assigned to Purchasing and usage responsibility assigned to the producing departments.

Just as two variances are computed for material (price, usage), two variances are computed for the other costs. The two variances are computed because costs incurred by the company can be controlled if the price paid and the quantity used are kept under control. Therefore, a price

Hypothetical Corporation
Data on Actual Production for
One-Month Period[a]

Department

Machining
Units produced 1,000 units
Cost charged to department
  Material (4,100 ft) $ 8,200
  Labor (2,100 actual hr) 11,000
  Overhead (8,300 actual machine hr) 6,000

$25,200

Grinding
Units produced 900 units
Costs charged to department
  Costs from Machining $19,800
  Material 1,300
  Labor (2,600 actual hr) 10,400
  Overhead 3,800

$35,300

Assembly
Units produced 1,000 units
Costs charged to department
  Costs from Grinding $38,500
  Material 13,000
  Labor (5,100 actual hours) 15,400
  Overhead
    Supervision $ 860
    Material handling 4,538
    Factory supplies 692
    Depreciation 200
    Maintenance 3,795 10,085

$76,985

Power and Heat
Total output 200,000 kWh
Total costs charged to department $12,000

Department		
Maintenance		
Maintenance labor		$ 4,560
Maintenance supplies		825
Depreciation		150
Supervision		940
		$ 6,475
Standard labor hours for work performed	700 hr	
Actual maintenance labor hours worked	750 hr	

ᵃ Assume that all units are completed and that there are no units in process at the end of the month.

Figure 6-4

variance and a usage variance are computed for material, labor, and overhead to pinpoint price or quantity factors that are out of control.

For example, the labor rate variance of $100 in the assembly department may indicate that excess overtime was worked or that a more expensive mix of workers was used. The meaning attached to this variance depends on the method used to establish departmental labor rate standards (e.g., overtime included or excluded from rate). The budget amount (standard) is computed by multiplying the standard labor hourly rate ($3) by the actual hours worked (5,100) to arrive at the price that should have been paid ($15,300) for the number of hours purchased. Comparison of the standard cost of $15,300 with the actual labor cost charged to Assembly provides the variance of $100. Because this variance is less than 1% of the budgeted amount, it is unlikely that the department supervisor will take action to reduce the labor rate of the workers under him.

The labor efficiency variance is developed by converting to a dollar amount the difference between the standard labor hours that should have been used and the actual number of hours used. For the assembly department, 5,000 hours (1,000 units produced × 5 hours per unit) should have been used, but 5,100 hours was actually used. The excess quantity of 100 hours is converted to a dollar amount using the standard rate of $3 an hour, for a total variance of $300. The budget amount shown in the assembly department report for the labor efficiency variance is developed by applying the standard labor rate of $3 to the standard labor hours of 5,000.

Hypothetical Corporation
Monthly Performance Report

Department: Assembly   Period: Month
Supervisor: G. Rind   Base: DLH

Expense	Budget	Variance
Cost from Grinding	$38,500	$ –0–
Material	12,000	(1,000)
Labor		
Rate	15,300	(100)
Efficiency	15,000	(300)
Total labor variance		(400)
Overhead		
Spending	9,995	(90)
Efficiency	9,825	(170)
Total overhead variance		(260)
Total variance		$(1,660)

Overhead Spending		
Supervision	$ 840	$ (20)
Material handling	4,548	10
Factory supplies	662	(30)
Depreciation	200	–0–
Maintenance	3,745	(50)
	$ 9,995	$ (90)

Figure 6-5

Overhead variances are computed in the same manner employed for developing variances for material and labor. However, the meaning of the overhead spending variance is different from that of the labor rate variance or the material price variance. The overhead spending variance results from a comparison of two amounts: the overhead amount that should have been charged to a department for the actual overhead units used, and the actual overhead amount charged to the department. The assembly department, as an illustration, should have incurred a total overhead cost of $9,995 for the 5,100 actual labor hours worked [(5,100 hours× $1.70) + $1,325). However, $10,085 was actually incurred in the assembly department, and this resulted in an overhead spending variance of $90. The variance may have been caused by price fluctuations in the overhead items used, as well as by variations in the quantity of the individual overhead items used. If all overhead expenses enter the accounting system at a standard price, the variance is due to usage; but if overhead expenses enter the system at actual cost, the variance is due to a combination of usage and price.

Regardless of whether the overhead expenses enter the system at standard or actual cost, the overhead spending variance has meaning for the department supervisor only if it is shown for each item of overhead expense. Accordingly, this variance is detailed for each item of overhead expense incurred in the assembly department. Since the budgeted amount of overhead for each expense item and the variance from the budget is listed, the departmental supervisor can readily identify overhead expense items that are causing problems. The budgeted amounts are computed by using the actual labor hours worked, together with the rate and amount budget for the assembly department.

Depreciation expense on equipment used in the assembly department represents one of the overhead expenses charged to that department. Some accountants insist that such an expense is beyond the control of the department supervisor because he does not decide when to purchase the equipment or what type of equipment to purchase. Therefore, these accountants argue, depreciation expense on equipment should be reported to the individual who purchases the machine instead of to the department supervisor. On the other hand, it can be argued that the department supervisor does influence the depreciation expense through the manner in which he uses his equipment. The depreciation expense represents a rough estimate of the service potential of the machine which has been consumed during a specific time period. If the supervisor, through improper maintenance or poor supervision of the workers using the machine, reduces the future services that can be provided by the machine, he has caused the depreciation cost to increase. This increase may not be apparent until a later period, but including the expense on his report emphasizes to the department supervisor that he is responsible for the efficient use of the equipment. Depreciation expense in this example, then, is included in the assembly department report to remind the department supervisor of his responsibility for the efficient utilization of the equipment.

The overhead efficiency variance that appears on the assembly report represents the excess cost or cost saving that results from using more or

Hypothetical Corporation
Monthly Performance Report

Department: Maintenance   Period: Month
Supervisor: I. Fixit   Base: Maintenance Labor
                                 Hours

	Budget	Variance
Maintenance efficiency	$6,000	$(350)
Maintenance spending	6,350	(125)
Maintenance spending in detail		
Maintenance labor	4,500	(60)
Maintenance supplies	800	(25)
Depreciation	150	–0–
Supervision	900	(40)
	$6,350	$(125)

Figure 6-6

fewer overhead units than the standard quantity. In the assembly department, overhead units are measured by direct labor hours; thus any usage of labor hours in excess of standard causes overhead expense to increase. In other words, excess labor hours not only increase labor expense in the assembly department, these extra hours also cause overhead expenses to increase at the rate of $1.70 an hour. The 100 labor hours worked in excess of the standard caused the company to incur $170 in excess overhead expenses. The overhead cost of $1.70 for each labor hour is the total of the rate column in the assembly department rate and amount budget.

Performance reports for the service departments include only two types of variances (efficiency and spending) because all service department costs are overhead costs by definition. The report for the maintenance department appears in Figure 6-6. The efficiency variance is computed by comparing the cost of the standard number of maintenance labor hours ($4,900) with the standard cost of the actual labor hours ($5,250), or by multiplying the extra 50 hours worked by the $7 rate in the maintenance department rate and amount budget. The $350 variance represents the extra cost incurred because of the inefficient use of maintenance labor, and the spending variance represents the extra expense incurred by the company because of price fluctuations or usage variances in the individual items of

overhead expense. The budgeted amount in the report is developed by applying the actual maintenance hours worked (750) to the total cost increase
for each additional maintenance labor hour worked ($7), which gives a
total variable maintenance cost of $5,250. The fixed monthly cost of $1,100
is added to this amount for a total budget amount of $6,350. As is true with
overhead expenses in producing departments, the individual elements of
overhead are listed for the benefit of the maintenance supervisor who can
see which expense items need attention.

The plant manager receives a report on the performance of the departments for which he is responsible. This report (Figure 6-7) provides a
concise summary of variances by department and by causal factor. For
example, by scanning the right-hand column, the plant manager can
quickly identify the departments that need attention. A look to the left of
the departmental total enables him to identify the factor causing the
trouble in a department. A glance at the departmental totals indicates that
there seem to be problems in the machining and assembly departments,
since Figure 6-7 reveals that variances for these departments are signifi-

Hypothetical Corporation
Monthly Performance Report

Department: Plant Manager No. 2   Period: Month
Supervisor: G. Getum

		Labor		Overhead		
Department	Usage	Rate	Efficiency	Spending	Efficiency	Total
Manager's office[a]	$ –0–	$ –0–	$ –0–	$ 200	$ –0–	$ 200
Machining	(200)	(500)	(500)	(350)	(150)	(1,700)
Grinding	50	–0–	400	–0–	100	550
Assembly	(1,000)	(100)	(300)	(90)	(170)	(1,660)
Power and heat	–0–	–0–	–0–	(1,000)	–0–	(1,000)
Maintenance	–0–	–0–	–0–	(125)	(350)	(475)
Total	$(1,150)	$(600)	$(400)	$(1,365)	$(570)	(4,085)
						89,240
Total budgeted cost						
Total actual cost						93,325

[a] Monthly budgeted expense is $1,200.

Figure 6-7

cantly larger than for the other departments. Within the machining department, where there are $500 rate and $500 efficiency variances, labor seems to be the most important problem. In the assembly department, the $1,000 material usage variance indicates that material usage is the big problem. For additional information on the departments that are experiencing difficulties, the plant manager can go to the reports for these departments to examine the detailed variances for each departmental cost element. For instance, the material usage variance is normally identified by individual type of material in the departmental report, although only the total variance is included in the report for the plant manager. In summary, the report for the plant manager is designed to identify departments that need attention and the troublesome cost category within each such department.

The total cost variances ($4,085) for the plant, when combined with the total budgeted cost for the plant ($89,240), provides the total actual cost incurred in the plant of $93,325. The total budgeted cost and the total actual cost cannot be calculated by merely adding the budgeted and actual costs for the individual departments because the cost transfers from one department to another must be taken into account. Maintenance cost, for instance, appears in the maintenance department report, and part of the same cost appears in the reports for the departments receiving maintenance services during the month. This apparent double counting of expenses occurs because the costs flow through several responsibility areas during the same month, and the cost is measured as it is charged to each department. Thus part of maintenance cost may flow to the machining department, where it is attached to the product and is then transferred to Grinding; from this department the cost may flow to Assembly, all during a one-month period. Consequently, if the costs charged to each department are totaled to arrive at a total cost for the plant, some costs will be counted several times, causing an erroneous total for plant expenses. Of course, this can be corrected by showing on each departmental report the total cost transferred. However, such a number adds no usable information to the report; besides, there is no compelling reason for having the summation of departmental report totals equal the totals for the plant. The departmental cost variances are additive because none of these are transferred from one department to another.

The report for the production vice-president (Figure 6-8) includes a summary of the variances for each plant and for the purchasing department. This report helps the vice-president to locate problems in the responsibility segments reporting to him, and it shows the total budget, total cost variances, and total actual production costs for the month. The total

Hypothetical Corporation
Monthly Performance Report

Period: Month

Department: Vice-President of Production
Supervisor: R. Smith

	Material		Labor		Overhead		Total
	Price	Usage	Rate	Efficiency	Spending	Efficiency	
Vice-president's office		$ –0–	$ –0–	$ –0–	$ (150)	$ –0–	$ (150)
Plant 1		(50)	(400)	(1,600)	(60)	(1,000)	(3,110)
Plant 2[a]		(1,150)	(600)	(400)	(1,365)	(570)	(4,085)
Purchasing	(800)	–0–	–0–	–0–	(300)	–0–	(1,100)
	$(800)	$(1,200)	$(1,000)	$(2,000)	$(1,875)	$(1,570)	$(8,445)

Total budgeted cost	
Plant 1	$300,000
Plant 2	89,240
Purchasing	3,000
Vice-president's office	3,393
	395,633
Total actual cost of production function	$404,078

[a] Total variances from plant manager's report in Figure 6-7.

Figure 6-8

83

production variances in this report indicate the amount by which the production function missed its expense target for the month, and the total variances for each of the segments reporting to the vice-president indicate the extent to which each responsibility area caused the production function to miss its target.

Specialized Reports

Several additional reports can be prepared for the vice-president and for other organization levels in the production function. For example, material price variances may be given in greater detail in a report like the one in Figure 6-9. This report shows price variances by material class, but only significant price variances are included. To eliminate the numerous items with small variances, this monthly report includes only 80% of the current dollar value of purchases.

Several types of special reports on labor efficiency can also be developed to pinpoint efficient and inefficient labor performance. The report in Figure 6-10 summarizes labor cost performance by production department for plant 16. This weekly report shows both hours and costs, and it supplies actual labor cost data for regular pay and for overtime and shift premiums to help identify the causes of variances between standard and actual labor cost. Also it shows the standard labor rate for each department and the actual labor rate for the labor costs charged to the department; this allows the plant manager to compare standard and actual costs for each department on an hourly basis.

A much more detailed comparison of standard and actual labor performance is provided by the system illustrated in Figure 6-11. This report shows labor efficiency by part number, but the operations detail for a part is printed by the computer only when labor efficiency for a part exceeds a range established by the department foreman. When it receives this kind of detail from the labor efficiency report, the company is able to learn why labor efficiency is deviating from standard for a particular part. If one employee caused the variance, that individual is quickly identified, as Jane Brown was in this report. If all workers deviate from the standard in the same direction, reevaluation of the standard is indicated for it may be inaccurate.

The report examples for Hypothetical Corporation are monthly performance reports, and the other sample reports were prepared on a monthly, weekly, or quarterly basis. In some cases, however, such as a job shop operation, reports may be prepared as key stages of a job are completed. That is, the reports are prepared for each job as work progresses on

Analysis of Price Variances for October

Account Number	Account Name	Purchases this Month	Variance this Month	Percentage of Variance to Purchase	Cumulative Change in Purchase	Percentage of Variance Since Last Standards Date
520	Steel	$ 78,400	$ 1,250	1.6	$ 675,800	1.5
521	Tubing	21,200	800	3.8	196,000	2.0
530	Bearings	42,700	2,800	6.6	384,000	3.4
532	Castings	68,300	1,400	2.0	637,000	2.1
534	Forgings	41,800	(900)	(2.2)	402,000	1.1
535	Brakes	18,900	(1,200)	(6.3)	167,000	(7.5)
536	Bulk parts	17,600	400	2.3	195,200	1.0
538	Screw machine	21,800	800	3.7	211,000	(.6)
539	Stampings	19,300	400	2.1	162,000	1.6
544	Other	67,400	(1,100)	(1.6)	512,000	0.2
		$397,400	$ 4,650	1.2%	$3,542,000	1.0

Source: "Development and Reporting of Variances," Accounting Practice Report Number 15, *NAA Bulletin* (formerly *Management Accounting*) (July 1962), Section 3, Vol. **43;** No. 11, p. 6.

Figure 6-9

Department: Plant 16
Supervisor: U. Weave

Nifty Carpet Company
Analysis of Actual and Standard Labor Cost

Period: Week 32

Department	Standard			Actual						Total Actual Labor Rate
	Hours	Rate	Cost	Hours	Rate	Regular Payroll	Overtime Premium	Shift Premium	Gross Payroll	
Warping	1,600	3.00	$ 4,800	1,700	3.00	$ 5,100	$ 600	$ 400	$ 6,100	3.59
Tufting	2,000	3.25	6,500	1,900	3.25	6,175	200	300	6,675	3.51
Oven	1,000	3.20	3,200	1,100	3.25	3,575	100	200	3,875	3.52
Shearing	2,200	3.10	6,820	2,200	3.10	6,820	200	100	7,120	3.24
Inspection	800	4.00	3,200	850	4.20	3,570	60	40	3,670	4.32
Total	7,600		$24,520	7,750		$25,240	$1,160	$1,040	$27,440	

Figure 6-10

86

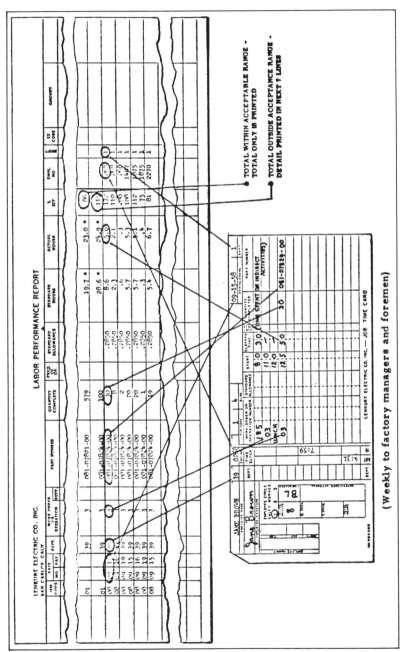

Figure 6-11 Sample labor performance report form. Source: National Association of Accountants, Accounting Practice Report 9, *Reports Which Management Find Most Useful*, 1960.

87

the job instead of as time passes. For example, a construction company may prepare performance reports on its various jobs as certain milestone points are reached on each job. The advantage of reporting according to job progress instead of according to time periods is that some of the problems of measuring degree of completion are avoided. When a report is prepared as the third floor steelwork is completed on an office building, it is relatively easy to verify that the steelwork for the third floor has been completed. Actual costs of completing the steelwork to this stage are then compared with the original cost estimate, which serves as the standard, to generate cost variances.

The same approach can be used in a job shop that builds custom products requiring several months or years to complete. Giant electric transformers or boilers for steam plants are products that are usually custom made, and the preparation of reports as work progresses furnishes meaningful cost information for the managers responsible for controlling the production costs. Of course, the use of work progress instead of time periods for reporting cost performance requires a few accounting adjustments. For example, supervisory salaries that are fixed for one month will vary with the length of the reporting period, and so will straight line depreciation. However, the effort required for these few accounting adjustments is far outweighed by the increased benefits derived from reporting cost performance on a work progress basis.

Actual Cost System

As noted in the opening pages of this chapter, cost control requires a standard against which actual cost can be compared to determine whether it is out of control. In an actual cost system, past performance can help provide a perspective on what the current cost level should be. Therefore, production performance reports for actual costs should always include data on costs for the prior month or for the same month from the previous year. Also, year-to-date data provide information that helps the decision maker formulate a standard he can use to evaluate the actual cost level.

The report in Figure 6-12 illustrates a format that can be used for a production department monthly report. This report shows the current month in relation to the same month for the previous year, and it does the same for the year-to-date amounts. The expenses for June seem to be reasonable when compared with previous year data, except for the expendable tools category. The expense of $200 for the current month is significantly higher than the $25 for the same month in the previous year. The year-to-date amounts follow a similar pattern, with a current year-to-date amount of $1,300 as compared with $600 for the previous year. Consequently, the department supervisor will probably investigate this expense item to see why there has been such an increase in the expense. In this case the comparative data help the supervisor to identify expenses that should be investigated, although comparative data are less precise than budget data for identifying expenses that are out of control.

A direct cost report for the factory manager is presented in Figure 6-13. As in the case of the company utilizing a standard cost system, this report contains a summary of departmental results for the factory. Total costs charged to each department are shown for the current month and for year-to-date for both the previous and the current years. Such comparative data for individual departments will help the plant manager locate the departments that seem to be having cost problems. Interdepartmental charges are eliminated at the bottom of this report to show total actual costs incurred in the plant. These charges are shown as a deduction on the report in an actual cost system because the emphasis is on the comparison of actual costs; they are not shown on the report in a standard cost system because the cost variances are the action messages, and these variances are not affected by interdepartmental cost charges.

Crossbow Metals, Inc.
Monthly Cost Report

Department: Drill Press   Period: June
Supervisor: R. Jones

Year to Date	Year to Date Last Year		This Month	This Month Last Year
$250,000	$230,000	Material	$40,000	$35,000
93,000	90,000	Labor	15,000	14,500
		Overhead		
4,200	4,000	Supervision	700	650
2,800	3,200	Material handling	500	625
1,100	1,000	Repair and rework	200	175
700	650	Training	100	150
3,000	2,500	Supplies	400	350
1,300	600	Expendable tools	200	25
2,200	2,400	Maintenance	400	375
$358,300	$334,350	Total direct department costs	$57,500	$51,850

Figure 6-12

Crossbow Metals, Inc.
Monthly Cost Report

Department: Plant Manager   Period: June
Supervisor: F. Reob

Year to Date	Year to Date Last Year		This Month	This Month Last Year
$ 29,500	$ 28,300	Manager's office	$ 4,900	$ 4,700
110,000	108,660	Punch press	29,400	30,300
106,000	103,340	Lathe	25,000	23,000
358,300	334,350	Drill press (Figure 6-12)	57,500	51,850
130,200	127,650	Assembly	42,300	41,050
132,000	125,000	Maintenance	21,000	20,100
(92,000)	(94,000)	Interdepartmental charges	(15,600)	(16,200)
$774,000	$733,300	Total plant expenses	$164,500	$154,800

Figure 6-13

In the actual direct cost system, just as in the standard direct cost system, each segment report includes only the costs that are controlled by the segment manager. No arbitrary cost allocations of administrative costs are made, and no service department fixed costs are transferred to producing departments.

In summary, the major difference between production performance reports in a standard direct cost system and in an actual direct cost system is in the cost variances provided by the standard cost system. Standard cost reports identify price and usage variances for all cost elements, whereas the emphasis in actual cost reports is on the provision of prior period amounts for comparison with current cost amounts.

CHAPTER 7

MARKET REPORTING SYSTEMS

A direct cost system provides relevant information for evaluating product, salesman, and territory performance; it identifies deviations from profit targets by organization segment and by product segment; and for each segment the system pinpoints the dollar deviation caused by price, cost, volume, and mix changes

BASIC CONCEPTS

The basic structure of the market reporting system is built on the concept of contribution reporting. This type of reporting system focuses management attention on the profit contribution produced by the various revenue generating segments. Each segment contributes to the results of the business, but only the business as a whole can earn a profit or sustain a loss. No meaningful profit or loss amount can be computed for a marketing segment; instead, the amount that the segment contributes to company results can be computed to show the impact on company profitability of the segment operations. This approach to marketing reports emphasizes upward contribution by market segments instead of downward cost allocations.

Because of this emphasis on segment contributions, the market segment manager is evaluated on the basis of how close his actual segment contribution is to the target contribution he is supposed to generate. In other words, the standard to which actual territory results are compared for control purposes is the target contribution amount that was developed when the annual profit plan was put together. This approach differs from that used in the cost control process, in which the standard cost for the actual output is computed after the actual output has been measured; then, to determine whether costs are under control, the actual costs are compared with what the cost for the actual output should have been. In the contribution control process, however, the actual contribution generated by a market segment is compared with a predetermined target that remains fixed at the planned amount. Of course the planned contribution may be shifted upward or downward as conditions change, but this change in the planned amount takes place as a result of a management decision, not an output measurement.

Contribution control also differs from cost control in the precision of the variance amounts developed by the two processes. Cost standards are developed from relatively objective measurements, and the standard cost for a given output is readily computed using these standards. In contrast, the target contribution amounts that are used as a standard for contribution control result from a judgment decision by company management. The planned contribution amount for a market segment represents the amount that, in the considered judgment of company managers, can be generated by that segment. Consequently, the precision of the contribution amount for variance computation purposes is much less than that of the cost standards used to compute production cost variances. The executive who receives a report containing both contribution and production cost variances should be aware that a dollar amount for a production variance does not have the same significance as an equal dollar amount for a contribution variance.

Because the market segment reports include only the factors that can be influenced by the segment manager with his decisions, no production cost variances are transferred to market segments. The costs of the products sold in the market segments are transferred to the appropriate segments at standard direct cost. By transferring direct product cost to the market segment, the accountant communicates to the marketing manager the dollar increase in total production costs required for a one-unit increase in sales. This information is very helpful to marketing managers who must analyze cost–volume–profit relationships to make decisions. Also, this procedure is in agreement with the concept of responsibility accounting; the marketing manager's decision to sell one more unit causes the production function to incur the costs of producing one more unit. If the unit of product is produced inefficiently, the cost variances that result are the responsibility of the production function. None of the variances are passed on to the marketing managers because the decisions that cause the production cost variances are made in the production function.

MARKETING COSTS

The costs that the marketing managers influence with their decisions can be classified into three groups: order getting costs, order filling costs, and market administration costs.

Order getting costs are incurred to persuade the customer to buy. Advertising, special promotions, and premiums are a few of the many costs incurred to persuade the customer to buy a company's product. The level of these costs is determined when the annual profit plan is developed, and the costs are budgeted in amounts that will generate the sales volume needed for the planned profit. That is, the company managers prepare spending plans for order getting costs in such a way that only the dollar expenditure necessary to produce the desired level of sales will be budgeted. The cost effectiveness of the amounts spent on order getting costs is an important consideration in planning expenditure levels, and control of these costs is exercised through periodic reports that show whether the planned amounts are being spent in the way originally scheduled. Actual expenditures that are less than the planned amount are carefully scrutinized by marketing executives because less spending on order getting costs usually means fewer sales.

Order filling costs are associated with delivering to the customer the product he has purchased. These are variable costs that vary with the unit or dollar amount of sales. Transportation costs are incurred as a result of the sale, packaging costs increase because a sale is made, and order processing costs are also caused by a sale. The planning and control of order filling costs, then, is very similar to the planning and control of production costs. Standards are established for the various costs, and forecast expense is computed by applying the standards to the forecast volume; control amounts are developed by applying the standards to the actual sales volume.

Transportation standards may be developed by using zip codes to compute the distance between warehouses and customers for transportation cost standards, or transportation cost may be stated as a percentage of sales. Packaging cost standards may be established for an average sales transaction, or these standards may also be established as a percentage of dollar sales.

Market administration costs are the costs incurred to coordinate marketing activities, and these costs consist largely of planned fixed costs. Costs of operating the office of the marketing vice-president and of the offices of the various territory managers are market administration costs. These costs are planned fixed costs, and the levels of these costs are established during the annual budget process.

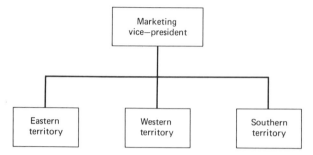

Figure 7-1   Hypothetical Corporation marketing organization chart.

MARKETING REPORTS

Marketing report systems, just like production report systems, are designed to fit the organization chart relevant for that function. For instance, the organization chart for the Hypothetical Corporation (Figure 7-1) shows three sales territories reporting to a marketing vice-president. Marketing performance reports are prepared for each of three sales territories, and a performance summary for the three territories is prepared for the marketing vice-president.

Before, performance reports can be developed for the individual territories, however, a marketing plan must be available. Figure 7-2 presents the data from which the marketing plan for Hypothetical Corporation is assembled. This illustration includes data on the following areas: budget plan for sales volume, order getting costs, order filling costs, administration costs, and production costs. The unit production cost for product Red is the same standard unit cost that appeared in Figure 5-3. In addition to the cost information, data are also furnished on standard selling prices. These standard selling prices are the dollar amounts for which the company intends to sell its products. Variances from these selling prices help point out excessive price cutting and indicate the profit effect of the price cuts.

The planning data are assembled in the form of a territory contribution plan in Figure 7-3, where the variable production and marketing costs are deducted from the planned revenue to arrive at marginal income. Next the territory contribution is computed by deducting the fixed administration and promotion costs that are direct to each territory from the territory marginal income. The territory fixed costs are direct fixed costs of the marketing territories; that is, the fixed expense amounts are directly traceable to the territories from whose marginal income they are deducted. As an illustration, consider the direct fixed costs of $8,100 for the Eastern Terri-

Hypothetical Corporation
Planned Marketing Activities for One Month

	Eastern Territory	Western Territory	Southern Territory
I. Sales territory plans			
Sales in units			
Red	1,000	500	1,200
Blue	300	200	100
Green	1,000	1,200	2,500
Promotion costs			
Red	$ 600	$ 400	$ 200
Blue	800	200	300
Green	1,200	200	500
Common to all products	2,000	3,000	4,000
Total	$4,600	$3,800	$5,000
Administration costs			
Rent	$2,000	$2,300	$4,000
Salaries	1,500	1,600	1,800
Total	$3,500	$3,900	$5,800

Standards
  Products cost standards
    Red $ 74
    Blue   60
    Green   50
  Marketing cost standards
    Sales commissions: 5% of dollar sales
    Transportation: 2% of dollar sales
  Standard selling prices
    Red $ 120
    Blue   90
    Green   100

II. Planned expenditures for marketing vice-president
    Administration costs $12,000
    Promotion expenditures   12,000
                             _____
                              24,000

Figure 7-2

tory. This amount includes administration costs of $3,500 (rent of $2,000, plus salaries of $1,500) and promotion costs of $4,600, both of which are controlled by the Eastern Territory manager. Because these expense amounts are controlled by the territory manager, they are considered along with the revenue he is responsible for generating.

In this example the territory manager is assumed to have the decision making authority to cause his fixed costs to increase or decrease. No home office cost allocations are included in his fixed costs. The common fixed costs that are direct to the marketing function but not traceable to any of the individual sales territories are then deducted from the total territory contribution to compute the total dollar amount of planned contribution for the marketing function. This amount of $267,240 (see Figure 7–3) is the contribution of the marketing function to corporate overhead and profits. The planned marketing contribution must be large enough to cover fixed production costs and corporate administrative costs or the company will operate at a loss.

Besides showing contribution by territory, the marketing plan frequently includes a schedule of contribution by product for each territory. Data on the planned product contribution for the three products sold in the Eastern Territory are presented in Figure 7-4. This example shows the revenue generated and direct costs incurred for each product. The direct fixed marketing costs consist of expenses, such as advertising, that are directly traceable to the individual products. In this case no fixed production costs are direct to any of the products sold. This is true because all products are sold in all territories, and any fixed costs that are direct to a specific product are common to the sales territories. The schedule of product contribution for a territory shows the territory manager the target contribution he should strive to attain for each of his products. However, his performance is usually evaluated on the basis of total territory contribution rather than on the contribution produced by each product.

After the marketing plan is accepted and approved, the territory managers attempt to meet the contribution targets for their respective territories. At the end of each month these managers are given performance reports revealing how well they have achieved their goals. The actual sales and costs for Hypothetical Corporation appear in Figure 7-5. The data represent the actual revenue and actual costs by territory; the details of the actual revenue and actual costs for the Eastern Territory are shown by product in Figure 7-6.

The transportation costs for the Eastern Territory is charged to each product at standard cost to arrive at an amount for product contribution; all the other costs, however, are shown at actual. Transportation expense is

Hypothetical Corporation
Planned Territory Contribution

Marketing Segment: Marketing Function   Period: Month
Manager: R. Smith, Marketing Vice-President

| | Total | Territory | | |
		Eastern	Western	Southern
Sales	$848,000	$247,000	$198,000	$403,000
Variable costs				
Production	470,800	142,000	109,000	219,800
Marketing				
Commissions	42,400	12,350	9,900	20,150
Transportation	16,960	4,940	3,960	8,060
	530,160	159,290	122,860	248,010
Marginal income	317,840	87,710	75,140	154,990
Direct fixed costs				
Administration				
Rent	8,300	2,000	2,300	4,000
Salaries	4,900	1,500	1,600	1,800
Promotion	13,400	4,600	3,800	5,000
	26,600	8,100	7,700	10,800
Territory contribution	291,240	$ 79,610	$ 67,440	$144,190
Common fixed costs				
Administration	12,000			
Promotion	12,000			
	24,000			
Total marketing function contribution	$267,240			

Figure 7-3

Hypothetical Corporation
Contribution by Products

Market Segment: Eastern Territory   Period: Month
Manager: J. Johnson

	Total	Product		
		Red	Blue	Green
Sales	$247,000	$120,000	$27,000	$100,000
Variable costs				
Production	142,000	74,000	18,000	50,000
Marketing—commissions	12,350	6,000	1,350	5,000
Marketing—transportation	4,940	2,400	540	2,000
	159,290	82,400	19,890	57,000
Marginal income	87,710	37,600	7,110	43,000
Direct fixed costs				
Production	–0–	–0–	–0–	–0–
Marketing	2,600	600	800	1,200
	2,600	600	800	1,200
Product contribution	85,110	$ 37,000	$ 6,310	$ 41,800
Territory direct fixed costs				
Administration	3,500			
Promotion	2,000			
	5,500			
Territory contribution	$ 79,610			

Figure 7-4

treated in this manner for the Eastern Territory because several of the products may be shipped to a customer in one shipment, and this makes transportation costs common to all the products shipped. Nevertheless, the transportation costs do increase because an additional unit of a product is sold, and the average amount of this increase (which is also the standard) is 2% of the standard unit sales price. Accordingly, each product is charged with the portion of the transportation expense that it caused the company to incur, even though in the accounting records actual transportation expense is detailed only at the territory level.

To develop performance reports for the sales territories, the accountant must prepare a work sheet such as the one in Figure 7-7 for the Eastern Sales Territory. This work sheet is used in arriving at variances that explain the difference between the planned territory contribution of $79,610 and the actual contribution of $70,500. The first column of the work sheet includes the marketing plan information developed in Figure 7-3. The "Control Budget" column amounts are computed through the multiplication of actual sales volume by the standard selling prices and standard production costs and through selection of the fixed cost amounts budgeted for the actual sales level. In most cases the planned fixed expenses and the "Control Budget" fixed expenses are the same; if some of the fixed costs include semifixed expenses, however, the budgeted expense for the actual sales volume may differ from that for the planned sales volume. In such cases, a cost variance appears on the marketing performance report.

The data in the "Actual Results" column are taken from the accounting records, and the last two columns are computed from the data in the first three. The "Volume/Mix" column is the difference between the first two columns, and the amounts in this column represent the differences between planned and actual contributions that are caused by changes from the budget plan in either the volume or the mix of products sold. The data in the "Price/Cost" column reveal the difference between the amounts in the "Control Budget" and the "Actual Results" columns. These amounts show how much actual revenue and actual costs deviated from what they should have been for the actual level of volume attained.

The data from this work sheet are used to prepare a territory performance report that pinpoints the reasons for the $9,110 difference between planned contribution of $79,610 and actual contribution of $70,500. This report (Figure 7-8) presents four variances that show the dollar amount of the contribution difference due to each of the four causal factors. The volume variance of $4,971 is computed through the multiplication of the planned marginal income ratio of .355101 by $14,000 (the amount by which "Control Budget" sales are less than planned sales). This $4,971 represents the marginal income that was lost by the Eastern Territory manager by selling at less than the planned volume. In a sense, it is the opportunity cost of not achieving the planned sales level. That is, by not selling at the planned sales volume, the company gave up $4,971 in marginal income.

The mix variance measures the impact on marginal income of selling a product mix different from the budget plan. This variance is computed through the multiplication of the sales amount in the "Control Budget"

Hypothetical Corporation
Actual Marketing Activities for One Month

	Total	Territory		
		Eastern	Western	Southern
Sales (units)				
Red	2,500	900	500	1,100
Blue	800	500	100	200
Green	3,700	800	1,300	1,600
Contribution for the month				
Sales				
Red	$302,000	$110,000	$ 60,000	$132,000
Blue	70,000	40,000	10,000	20,000
Green	358,000	81,000	122,000	155,000
	730,000	231,000	192,000	307,000
Variable costs				
Production	418,000	136,600	108,000	173,400
Marketing—commissions	36,500	11,550	9,600	15,350
Marketing—transportation	14,730	4,750	3,840	6,140
	469,230	152,900	121,440	194,890
Marginal income	260,770	78,100	70,560	112,110
Direct fixed costs				
Administration				
Rent	8,300	2,000	2,300	4,000
Salaries	5,000	1,600	1,700	1,700
Promotion	10,500	4,000	4,200	2,300
	23,800	7,600	8,200	8,000
Territory contribution	236,970	$ 70,500	$ 62,360	$104,110
Common fixed costs				
Administration	12,000			
Promotion	10,000			
Total contribution	$214,970			

Actual promotion expenditures, Eastern Territory

Expenditures direct to products	
Red	$ 300
Blue	800
Green	1,000
	$2,100
Expenditures common to all products	1,900
Total	$4,000

Figure 7-5

column ($233,000) by the difference (.011367) between the marginal income ratios for the first two columns. The $2,649 variance indicates that a product mix less profitable than originally planned was sold during the month.

The amount that remains after the volume and the mix variances have been deducted from the planned contribution indicates how much contribution should have been generated by the actual sales volume. However, price cuts and excessive expenditures on marketing costs in the Eastern Territory caused actual contribution to be less than it should have been. The prices in the Eastern Territory were cut by $2,000, but in cutting selling prices the salesmen also cut their commissions by $100. This caused a net sales price variance of $1,900. The cost variances are listed in detail on the report; thus the territory manager can see the dollar amount of the variances for each expense for which he is directly responsible.

The performance reports in Figure 7-8 helps the Eastern Territory manager identify the causes for his poor territory performance for the month. If he wants to know which product is causing most of his problems, however, he will review a report like the one in Figure 7-9, which gives him volume, price, and cost variances for each product or product line. A glance at this report will tell the Eastern Territory manager that product Green, with its $8,600 unfavorable volume variance, is responsible for most of his problems. Next in importance is product Red, whose unfavorable volume variance of $3,760 was partially offset by price increases of $1,900.

The territory manager is not the only individual in the company who receives information on marketing variances; the marketing vice-president is also vitally interested in marketing performance. Since he is indirectly responsible for the direct costs and revenues of the sales territories, he

Hypothetical Corporation
Territory Contribution Report

Market Segment: Eastern Sales Territory
Manager: J. Johnson

Period: Month

	Territory Total	Product		
		Red	Blue	Green
Sales	$231,000	$110,000	$40,000	$81,000
Variable costs				
Production	136,600	66,600	30,000	40,000
Marketing				
Commissions	11,550	5,500	2,000	4,050
Transportation (at standard)	4,660	2,160	900	1,600
	152,810	74,260	32,900	45,650
Product marginal income	78,190	35,740	7,100	35,350
Transportation cost variances	(90)			
Territory marginal income	78,100			
Direct fixed costs, Promotion	2,100	300	800	1,000
Product contribution		$ 35,440	$ 6,300	$34,350
Territory contribution before deducting territory direct fixed costs	76,000			
Territory direct fixed costs				
Administration				
Rent	2,000			
Salaries	1,600			
Promotion	1,900			
	5,500			
Territory contribution	$ 70,500			

Figure 7-6

receives a variance summary like the one in Figure 7-10. This report summarizes territory performance in the right-hand column, and it summarizes variances by type on the bottom line. Not only does the report show that actual contribution is $52,270 less than planned, but it also reveals which territory was responsible and what factor in the territory led to the poor performance. The Southern Territory showed the weakest performance in

Hypothetical Corporation
Marketing Performance Report Worksheet

Market Segment: Eastern Sales Territory   Period: Month
Manager: J. Johnson

	Budget Plan	Control Budget	Actual Results	Variance Volume/ Mix	Variance Price/ Cost
Sales	$247,000	$233,000	$231,000	$(14,000)	$(2,000)
Variable costs					
Production	142,000	136,600	136,600	5,400	–0–
Marketing					
Commissions	12,350	11,650	11,550	700	100
Transportation	4,940	4,660	4,750	280	(90)
	159,290	152,910	152,900	6,380	10
Marginal income	87,710	80,090	78,100	(7,620)	(1,990)
Marginal income percentage	.355101	.343734			
Direct fixed costs					
Administration					
Rent	2,000	2,000	2,000	–0–	–0–
Salaries	1,500	1,500	1,600	–0–	(100)
Promotion	4,600	4,600	4,000	–0–	600
	8,100	8,100	7,600	–0–	500
Territory contribution	$ 79,610	$ 71,990	$ 70,500	$ (7,620)	$(1,490)

Figure 7-7

Hypothetical Corporation
Marketing Variance Report

Market Segment: Eastern Sales Territory   Period: Month
Manager: J. Johnson

Planned territory contribution for month		$79,610
Volume variance		
Decrease in marginal income from a $14,000 reduction		
in sales ($14,000 × .355101)	$(4,971)	
Mix variance (.011367 × $233,000)	(2,649)	(7,620)
Standard marginal income for actual sales volume		71,990
Price variance		
Reduction in selling prices	(2,000)	
Less reduction in sales commissions	100	(1,900)
Cost variances		
Variable costs: transportation	(90)	
Fixed costs		
Salaries	(100)	
Promotion	600	410
Actual territory contribution for month		$70,500

Figure 7-8

this example, with $40,080 of unfavorable variances, and most of this variance was caused by the unfavorable sales variance of $35,766. With this information, the vice-president can quickly identify the territory and the factor in the territory causing the problem. In his discussion with the Southern Territory manager, a product variance report like the one for the Eastern Territory can be used to further pinpoint the source of the poor performance.

Although no salesman performance reports are included in this example, reports could be generated for each salesman in the same way that reports were prepared for the territories. Each territory manager would then receive a summary report of the variances for the salesmen reporting to him; and, in turn, the territories would be summarized in a report for the vice-president. The product variance reports would be especially helpful to

Hypothetical Corporation
Product Variance Report

Market Segment: Eastern Sales Territory Period: Month
Manager: J. Johnson

	Red	Blue	Green
Planned product contribution	$37,000	$6,310	$41,800
Volume variance	(3,760)	4,740	(8,600)
Price variance	1,900	(4,750)	950
Cost variance: promotion cost	300	–0–	200
Actual product contribution	$35,440	$6,300	$34,350

Figure 7-9

Hypothetical Corporation
Marketing Variance Report

Market Segment: Vice President of Marketing Period: Month
Manager: R. Smith

Market Segment	Variances				
	Volume	Mix	Price	Cost	Total
Eastern	$ (4,971)	$(2,649)	$ (1,900)	$ 410	$ (9,110)
Western	1,550	380	(6,650)	(360)	(5,080)
Southern	(35,766)	(4,324)	(2,850)	2,860	(40,080)
Vice-president's office	–0–	–0–	–0–	2,000	2,000
	$(39,187)	$(6,593)	$(11,400)	$4,910	$(52,270)
Total planned contribution					267,240
Total actual contribution					$214,970

Figure 7-10

salesmen who are deciding how to redirect their selling efforts to meet their contribution targets.

In companies selling many different products (e.g.,department stores) the contribution performance reports present a problem because of the data collection difficulties. A department store, for example, will usually find it difficult to keep track of every unit of every type of product sold, and the same is true of the wholesaler who sells thousands of different products. However, the data collection efforts can be drastically reduced if the company is willing to sacrifice some precision in its contribution reports.

For example, items in a department within a store can be grouped into three or four categories, with all items in a category being treated as if they were precisely the same. A weighted average standard selling price and a weighted average standard cost for each category can be computed. These standards are then multiplied by forecast or actual volume to produce the numbers required by the contribution variance work sheet. The approach requires that data on the units sold in each category be collected, but this is seldom an insurmountable task. In fact, in some cases the number of units transferred into a department during a month can be used as a surrogate for the units sold. This works in grocery stores in which departmental turnover is so high that beginning and ending inventories are relatively insignificant in relation to sales.

In using this approach to simplifying data collection, the accountant has a problem in determining how many categories to establish. If a small number of categories are used, data collection is simple and efficient, but the resulting reports may be so condensed that the information in them is useless for decision making. On the other hand, if numerous categories are established with an increase in data collection costs, the information in the reports becomes more useful to decision makers. Consequently, the accountant will have to attempt to achieve the optimum balance between data collection costs and report usefulness.

MONTHLY PERFORMANCE SUMMARIES

Not only do direct cost data supply relevant decision making information to company segment managers, they also provide the foundation for meaningful performance reporting for the company as a whole. For example, a combination of the data in the production vice-president's report in Figure 6-8 and the marketing vice-president's report in Figure 7-10 summarizes monthly performance for the company president and shows how much target net income was missed. Furthermore, the report indicates who should be questioned about the reasons for missing the target. Such a report (Figure 7-11) enables the company president to readily identify the problem areas in the organization and the factor in the troublesome segment that is causing the difficulty. It also shows the planned before-tax profit and the actual amount of profit earned, thus giving some perspective on the relative significance of the variances.

If the executive receiving the report illustrated in Figure 7-11 wants more detail about the marketing variances, he can refer to the marketing vice-president's report (Figure 7-10), and he might even examine the individual territory reports for specific information about which product is causing the problem. In other words, the report linkage provided by the responsibility reporting system enables the top executive to move as far down in the organization as necessary to obtain answers to his questions.

Another useful characteristic of the performance summary made possible by a direct cost system is the absence of income fluctuations due to changes in inventory levels. Because all inventory costs are variable costs, increases

Hypothetical Corporation
Monthly Performance Report

Segment: Company President   Period: Month
Manager: J. Jones

	Production	Marketing	Administration	Total
Material variances	$(2,000)			$ (2,000)
Labor variances	(3,000)			(3,000)
Production overhead variances	(3,445)			(3,445)
Volume variances		$(39,187)		(39,187)
Mix variances		(6,593)		(6,593)
Price variances		(11,400)		(11,400)
Cost variances		4,910	$(5,000)	(90)
Total	$(8,445)	$(52,270)	$(5,000)	$(65,715)
Planned before-tax income				67,000
Actual before-tax income				$1,285

Figure 7-11

or decreases in inventory do not delay or accelerate the charging of fixed expenses against income. Under direct costing, all fixed production costs are charged against revenue each month as a period cost—a cost that is incurred regardless of the level of production.

CONTRIBUTION REPORTS WITHOUT STANDARDS

Lack of production and marketing standards should not prevent a company from taking advantage of the benefits offered by direct costing. Market segment reports can still be prepared, and these reports can be pyramided upward in a responsibility reporting system. Without a marketing plan or marketing standards, however, the reports are limited to a disclosure of actual contribution for the segment. No contribution variances can be computed. Reports under these conditions would look much like the actual data presented in Figure 7-5. Since there would also be data for the month and for the year-to-date, the report recipient could gain some perspective on the current month's performance.

To make these reports on actual contribution more timely, the accountant should use some average of past production costs in preparing the material. This average can be adjusted quarterly to reflect recent events, and the precision lost in computing segment contribution with the average is readily offset by the increased usefulness of timely reports.

CHAPTER 8

COST—VOLUME—PROFIT ANALYSIS

One of the analytical planning tools that helps managers to evaluate the profit impact of alternative combinations of prices and costs is cost–volume–profit analysis. This tool works well with a direct cost system because such a system identifies costs by behavior pattern and segment responsibility. Consequently, no laborious and lengthy cost study is needed to identify total company fixed costs each time a company-wide cost–volume–profit analysis is wanted. Furthermore, managers of revenue generating segments can easily evaluate the contribution impact of different combinations of prices, promotion costs, and sales volume.

Product managers, territory sales managers, and individual salesmen can also use cost–volume–profit analysis to find answers to many questions that require fast answers. Questions such as the following can be readily answered with cost-volume-profit analysis techniques.*

1. How many units must be sold to earn a specified amount of profit? To break even?
2. How much will a revenue generating segment contribute to overall profit?
3. What will net profit be if a given sales volume is realized?
4. What will happen to profits if prices are increased? Decreased?
5. Will additional advertising be profitable?
6. What is the profit impact of changes in company cost structure?

The data, such as unit cost and direct segment fixed costs used to answer these questions, are readily available in the standard product cost records and in the segment budgets. If a company employs actual instead of standard costs, recent cost data are used to compute an average unit cost; data on marginal income ratios and revenue generating segment fixed costs can be taken from the most recent segment contribution reports. Thus collecting the data for cost–volume–profit analysis in an actual cost system

---

* National Association of Accountants, *Current Application of Direct Costing*, Research Report 37, New York: National Association of Accountants, January 1, 1961).

is more time-consuming than for a standard cost system, but this effort is still far less than required by an absorption cost system.

Although data collection for cost–volume–profit analysis is relatively easy in a direct cost system, the accountant who uses this tool must keep in mind that it does have some limitations. First of all, the analysis presents a highly simplified framework for looking at a complex process. For example, the accountant who prepares a cost–volume–profit analysis of a problem assumes that price and cost remain constant and that volume is the only factor that can vary. Competitive reaction to changes in the volume of goods sold by the company and possible cost changes at different levels of output are ignored.

Yet this simplicity, through its isolation of one factor for analysis, is also one of the strengths of cost–volume–profit analysis. It allows an accountant or manager to focus his attention on the profit impact of price and cost changes; he can then use his judgment to adjust the results of the analysis for possible changes in competitor activity or in cost relationships.

The cost behavior patterns used in cost–volume–profit analysis are linear. That is, the unit cost is assumed to be constant throughout the range of activity under consideration, and the fixed costs are assumed to be constant for the time period covered by the analysis. Semifixed expenses can cause problems if the accountant does not watch carefully the volume levels at which costs shift up or down. The analysis is relevant only so long as the semifixed expenses do not move from one step to another. For example, in computing a break-even passenger load for a shuttle flight, the accountant must recognize that the fixed cost for a passenger volume from zero to the capacity of one plane is lower than that for a passenger volume that requires more than one plane.

A linear total cost relationship also means that unit variable costs remain constant, and this assumption is valid for most cases in which production remains within the normal range of production activity. If production volume exceeds the normal range of production, unit costs may be higher than the unit cost used in the analysis. The same is true for activity levels below the normal range; unit costs may increase as output drops because of plant inefficiencies at low volume.

The mix of products sold must also be considered. Cost-volume-profit analysis assumes that the mix of products sold by the company, or by one of its segments, remains constant throughout the normal range of output. If the mix of products varies at different volume levels, the accountant must recognize that his analysis is faulty at the volumes at which the mix changes. This problem, which is illustrated later in the chapter, is mentioned here to emphasize that it is an essential assumption of cost–volume–profit analysis.

The product mix assumption and the cost relationship assumptions are illustrated in the break-even chart of Figure 8-1. This chart provides one means of analyzing cost–volume–profit relationships. The horizontal line at the $20 level represents fixed costs that remain constant for the entire range of activity under consideration. The dotted line that begins at the origin represents the total variable costs that increase in direct proportion to increases in output (i.e., variable cost per unit remains constant). The total cost line is simply the vertical summation of the variable and fixed cost lines.

The revenue line is a 45° line drawn from the origin, and the point at which it crosses the total cost line represents the break-even point. The cross-hatched area to the left of the break-even point includes the volume levels at which the revenue line is below total costs; at these volume levels

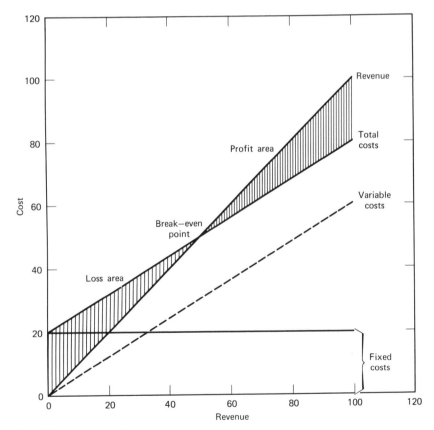

Figure 8-1   Break-even chart.

Sales	$100
Variable costs	60
Marginal income	40
Marginal income percentage	40%
Fixed costs	20
Profit	$ 20

$$\text{Break-even point} = \frac{\text{fixed costs}}{\text{marginal income percentage}} = \frac{20}{.40} = \$50$$

Margin of safety
  1. Dollar amount

Budgeted sales	$100
Break-even sales	50
Margin of safety	$ 50

  2. Percentage

$$\frac{\text{dollar margin of safety}}{\text{budgeted sales}} = \frac{\$50}{\$100} = 50\%$$

Margin of safety	50%

Figure 8-2

the company operates at a loss. To the right of the break-even point the revenue line is above the cost line, and the company earns a profit at these volume levels.

Another measure that can be related to the break-even chart is called the margin of safety. This measure indicates the dollar amount or percentage by which planned sales exceed the breakeven point. For example, assume that $100 of sales is planned for the graph illustrated in Figure 8-1. The margin of safety is $50, the amount by which the planned sales of $100 exceed the break-even point of $50. This computation and the percentage margin of safety appear in Figure 8-2.

The margin of safety tells roughly how much planned sales may decline before losses are incurred. A low margin of safety usually indicates that management should attempt to increase sales volume, increase selling prices, or reduce costs.

Some accountants and managers criticize the break-even chart because of its emphasis on breaking even; these individuals want the analysis to emphasize profits instead of break-even points. Accordingly, the so-called profit graph has been developed, and the sample in Figure 8-3 reveals the elements of such a graph. In constructing the profit graph, a break-even line is drawn parallel to the horizontal axis and a profit line is drawn from a point on the vertical axis equal to the loss incurred at zero sales volume (fixed costs). The slope of the profit line is determined by the marginal income ratio (i.e., the higher the marginal income ratio the steeper the slope, and vice versa). Thus the impact of changes in the marginal income ratio

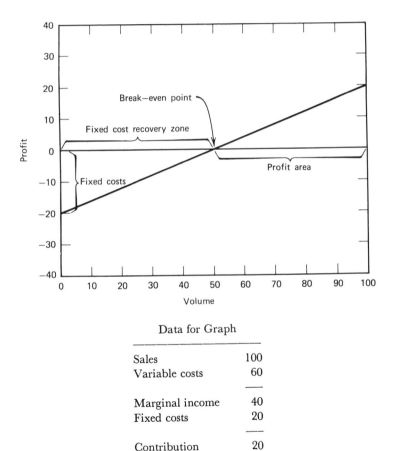

Data for Graph

Sales	100
Variable costs	60
Marginal income	40
Fixed costs	20
Contribution	20

Figure 8-3

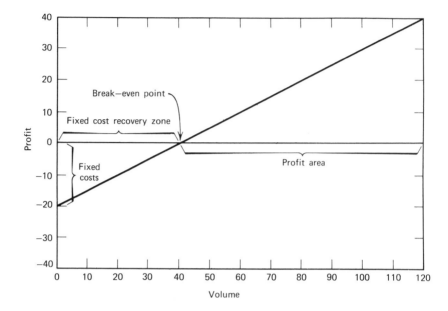

Data for Graph

Sales	120
Variable costs	60
Marginal income	60
Fixed costs	20
Contribution	40

Figure 8-4

on the break-even point and on profits can be easily demonstrated with the profit graph by changing the slope of the profit line.

The area to the left of the break-even point in this graph represents the volume levels at which marginal income is less than fixed costs. To the right of the break-even point is the profit area, and the amount of profit is measured by the vertical distance between the break-even line and the profit line. This graph is easier to read than the break-even graph because only two lines are on the graph.

Figure 8-4 demonstrates the effect on the graph of high marginal income ratios. The slope of the profit line is steeper in Figure 8-4 than in Figure 8-3 because the percentage of marginal income is 50% in Figure 8-4 and only 40% in Figure 8-3: The steeper the profit line, the lower the break-even point, and vice versa.

The effect of fixed cost changes is illustrated in Figure 8-5. Here the fixed costs have increased 50% above the fixed costs that were present in Figure 8-3. The former profit line is indicated by the dashed line, and the new profit line is parallel to the former one; the distance between the two is equal to the increase in fixed costs. The new break-even point has increased from $50 to $75, an increase of 50%. This is the same percentage increase as the increase in fixed costs; in fact, the new break-even point will always change by the same percentage as the percentage change in fixed costs.

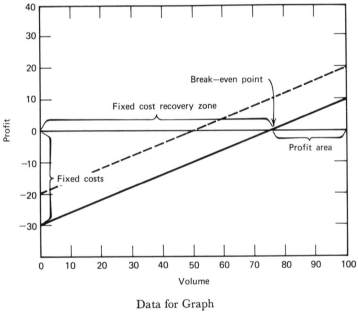

Data for Graph

Sales	100
Variable costs	60
Marginal income	40
Fixed costs	30
Contribution	10

Figure 8-5

The break-even chart and the profit graph are most fruitfully employed as a means of presenting financial information in a graphical form. These graphs provide a readily understood picture of cost–volume–profit relationships for decision makers who are uncomfortable with numbers. Or, even if the decision makers enjoy working with numerical analyses, the graphical presentation of data furnish a useful summary of the significant relationships.

For instance, if fixed costs are high, volume fluctuations usually result in wide fluctuations in profit. On the other hand, a business with low fixed costs generally experiences narrower swings in profit, as volume varies, than the firm with high fixed costs. Both these relationships can be concisely demonstrated by shifting the lines on the graph.

If a company with fixed costs wants to improve profits, it can attempt to reduce fixed expenses or to increase sales volume. Reduction of committed fixed costs requires long-range planning, but planned fixed expenses can be reduced in the short run if declining profits make such a move necessary. However, it must be remembered that low fixed costs do not of themselves indicate a good profit structure, for some of the most important approaches to cost reduction require fixed cost increases to reduce variable costs or to increase revenue.

USES OF COST–VOLUME–PROFIT ANALYSIS

As noted in an earlier paragraph, cost–volume–profit analysis can be used for short-term planning decisions that affect revenue generating segments as well as for those planning decisions that affect the entire company.* Therefore, the data from the marketing plan for the Eastern Sales Territory (Figure 7-3) of the Hypothetical Corporation, which served as a budget plan in Chapter 7, serves here to demonstrate how a sales territory manager can use cost–volume–profit analysis. These data are presented in the first section of Figure 8-6.

One amount that the territory manager might find useful is the territory break-even point, which is computed in the second section of Figure 8-6: $22,810 indicates the dollar amount of sales necessary to cover the direct fixed costs of the Eastern Territory. If sales for the territory fall below this amount, the company will be better off financially if it eliminates the territory. Thus the territory manager can use the break-even sales figure for

---

* For a discussion of the many uses of cost–volume–profit analysis, see the References at the end of the chapter.

computing his margin of safety after he has developed his territory sales plan.

However, a more worthwhile use of cost–volume–profit analysis consists of computing the territory dollar sales volume required for various target contribution amounts. Often companies establish minimum contribution targets for revenue generating segments. For instance, assume that the Hypothetical Corporation sets a minimum contribution of $40,000 for the Eastern Territory. The sales volume required to generate a contribution in this amount is computed in the third section of Figure 8-6; the dollar amount is $135,454. This sales amount can be used to calculate a number, similar to the margin of safety, that shows the amount by which planned

Hypothetical Corporation

---

1. Data from Eastern Territory marketing plan (Figure 7-3)

Sales	$247,000
Variable costs	159,290
Marginal income	87,710
Marginal income percentage	.355101
Direct fixed costs	8,100
Planned territory contribution	$ 79,610

2. Territory break-even point

$$\frac{\text{direct fixed costs}}{\text{marginal income percentage}} = \frac{\$8,100}{.355101} = \$22,810$$

3. Sales required for target contribution
   a. Target contribution $ 40,000

$$\frac{\text{direct fixed costs} + \text{target contribution}}{\text{marginal income percentage}} = \frac{\$8,100 + \$40,000}{.355101}$$

$$= \frac{\$48,100}{.355101} = \$135,454$$

   b. Target contribution $ 60,000

$$\frac{\$8,100 + \$60,000}{.355101} = \frac{\$68,100}{.355101} = \$191,776$$

Figure 8-6

1. Data from Hypothetical Corporation marketing plan for Eastern Territory for one month (Figure 7-4)

	Total	Product Red	Blue	Green
Sales	$247,000	$120,000	$27,000	$100,000
Variable costs	159,290	82,400	19,890	57,000
Marginal income	87,710	37,600	7,110	43,000
Marginal income percentage		.313333	.263333	.430000
Direct product fixed costs	2,600	600	800	1,200
Product contribution	85,110	$ 37,000	$ 6,310	$ 41,800
Direct territory fixed costs	5,500			
Territory contribution	$ 79,610			

2. Sales prices increased $10 for each product; variable costs remain at previous level

	Product Red	Blue	Green
New sales price	$130.00	$100.00	$110.00
Variable costs			
Production	74.00	60.00	50.00
Marketing	9.10	7.00	7.70
Total	83.10	67.00	57.70
Marginal income for each unit	46.90	33.00	52.30
Marginal income percentage	.360769	.330000	.475454

3. Dollar sales volume required to maintain previous product contribution level

	Red	Blue	Green
Target contribution	$ 37,000	$ 6,310	$ 41,800
Direct fixed costs	600	800	1,200
Marginal income required	37,600	7,110	43,000
	÷	÷	÷
Marginal income percentage for new prices	.360769	.330000	.475454
Required dollar sales volume	$104,260	$21,500	$ 90,420
Required sales in units	802	215	822

4. Sales prices decreased $10 for each product; variable costs remain at previous level

	Red	Blue	Green
New sales price	$110.00	$80.00	$90.00
Variable costs			
Production	74.00	60.00	50.00
Marketing	9.10	7.00	7.70
Total	83.10	67.00	57.70
Marginal income for each unit	26.90	13.00	32.30
Marginal income percentage	.244545	.162500	.358889

5. Dollar sales volume required to attain original contribution target

	Red	Blue	Green
Target contribution	$ 37,000	$ 6,310	$ 41,800
Direct fixed costs	600	800	1,200
	37,600	7,110	43,000
	÷	÷	÷
Marginal income percentage for reduced prices	.244545	.162500	.358889
Required dollar sales volume	$153,780	$43,760	$119,790
Required sales in units	1,398	547	1,331

Figure 8-7

sales exceed the minimum acceptable sales for the territory. The sales plan presented in Figure 7-3 showed planned sales of $247,000, and the minimum acceptable sales amount is $135,454; thus the sales plan is $111,546 above the minimum acceptable amount.

Assume that the territory manager is now notified that the company is revising the minimum acceptable contribution amounts for its sales territories, the new minimum for the Eastern Territory being set at $60,000. The territory manager can quickly compute the new minimum acceptable sales level. He simply adds the minimum territory contribution to the territory direct fixed costs to compute total marginal income required; then he divides this total by the marginal income percentage. All these data are readily available, thanks to the data classification provided by the direct cost system. The last computation in Figure 8-6 shows the new minimum acceptable sales level: $191,776.

The territory manager can use cost–volume–profit analysis in still other ways to develop the market plan for his sales territory. He can use the technique to evaluate price changes, for example. The planned monthly product contribution for each of the three products sold in the Eastern Territory was presented in Figure 7-4, and it is also included in the first section of Figure 8-7. The territory manager can use these data to evaluate the effect of product price changes.

In the second part of Figure 8-7, the selling price for each of the products is increased by $10, and the territory manager wants to see what dollar amount of sales is required at the new price to generate the same planned product contribution of $85,110. These computations appear in sections 2 and 3 of Figure 8-7. First a new marginal income percentage is computed for each product; this new percentage is next divided into the desired product marginal income, to arrive at the dollar sales required from each product. The number of units of each product that must be sold is also computed, and the territory manager is then in a position to make a judgment about whether the required units can be sold at the increased price.

For a price decrease, the same procedure is followed. The computations for a unit price decrease of $10 are illustrated in sections 4 and 5 of Figure 8-7. Here the required unit sales for each product are especially important because the cost–volume–profit computations may result in unit sales that are greater than the sales territory can absorb. In such a case, the territory manager can consider other means of increasing product contribution—such as increased promotion, selected price cuts, or increased emphasis on a more profitable mix of products. He may weigh various combinations of price increases, price decreases, and changes in promotion expenditures before arriving at the marketing plan for his territory. Regardless of the pricing or advertising strategy he chooses, the territory manager can evaluate the contribution impact of his strategy with cost–volume–profit techniques.

The marketing vice-president can perform the same types of analyses for the entire marketing function. For instance, he can use the data from the market plan for the company (see section 1 of Figure 8-8) to assess the impact on contribution of various changes in national advertising. A $10,000 increase in monthly advertising will require additional monthly sales of $26,680; a $20,000 monthly advertising increase will require a $53,360 monthly sales increase. The marketing vice-president can consult with his sales managers and market researchers to see whether sales increases above these amounts can be expected if the advertising is increased. In this case, the cost–volume–profit analysis allows a decision maker to approximate the minimum amount by which sales must increase to break even on the additional advertising expenditure.

In computing the sales amounts required to break even on the added advertising expenditures, the marketing vice-president assumed that the sales mix would not change. He could take into account sales mix changes by estimating the sales increases that will occur in each of the territories because of the added advertising. The third section of Figure 8-8 illustrates this approach. The sales increase expected in each territory from the $30,000 monthly increase in advertising is used to compute the additional marginal income expected from each territory. The added marginal income of $44,625 can then be compared with the $30,000 increase in advertising to determine whether the added expenditure should be made. Of course, this analysis assumes that the sales mix will remain constant in each territory.

If .374811, the marginal income percentage for the company, is used to estimate the additional marginal income produced by the $120,000 sales, the marginal income amount forecast is higher than that for the individual territories. This difference is caused by a change in the sales mix; almost half of the additional sales ($50,000) are generated by the Eastern Territory, which has a marginal income ratio of only .355101 as compared with the composite ratio for the company of .374811. Because of the distortions that product mix changes can cause in a cost–volume–profit analysis, the accountant should always examine his product mix assumptions when computations are made for various input combinations.

Another application of cost–volume–profit analysis deals with the decisions that result in changes in the company cost structure. To illustrate this use of the techniques, assume that the cost data presented in Figure 5-3 are for product Red. Assume further that these data represent the costs (except

1. Data from Hypothetical Corporation marketing plan for the month (Figure 7-3)

	Total	Eastern	Western	Southern
			Territory	
Sales	$848,000	$247,000	$198,000	$403,000
Variable costs	530,160	159,290	122,860	248,010
Marginal income	317,840	87,710	75,140	154,990
Marginal income percentage	.374811	.355101	.379495	.384591
Direct fixed costs	26,600	8,100	7,700	10,800
Territory contribution	291,240	$ 79,610	$ 67,440	$144,190
Common fixed costs	24,000			
Marketing contribution	$267,240			

2. Marketing vice-president plans to increase national advertising
   a. Advertising increased $10,000 monthly:

$$\text{sales increase required} = \frac{\text{advertising increase}}{\text{marginal income percentage}} = \frac{\$10,000}{.374811} = \$26,680$$

   b. Advertising increased $20,000 monthly: $20,000/.374811 = \$53,360$

3. National advertising increased $30,000, resulting in the following territory sales increases:

Eastern	$ 50,000
Western	10,000
Southern	60,000
Total	$120,000

Additional marginal income from sales increases:

Eastern	$50,000 × .355101 =	$17,755
Western	10,000 × .379495 =	3,795
Southern	60,000 × .384591 =	23,075
Total		$44,625

Additional marginal income, assuming no change in sales mix:
   sales increase × marginal income percentage
   $120,000 × .374811 = $44,977

Figure 8-8

I. Product Red: current production facility
   A. Standard cost (Figure 5-8) $74

   B. Monthly budgeted fixed costs of plant 1

Production departments (Figure 5-3)	
Machining	$ 1,500
Grinding	1,200
Assembly	1,325
Service departments (Figure 5-3)	
Power and Heat	10,000
Maintenance	1,100
Administration	25,000
Total monthly fixed costs	$ 40,125

II. Product Red: automated equipment installed in grinding department
   A. Standard cost (labor cost reduced $10 in Grinding) $64

   B. Monthly budgeted fixed costs of plant 1

Production Departments	
Machining	$ 1,500
Grinding	4,200
Assembly	1,325
Service departments	
Power and heat	10,000
Maintenance	1,100
Administration	25,000
Total cost	$ 43,125

   C. Monthly product contribution prior to installation of automated equipment in grinding department. These data were compiled from the marketing plan outlined in Figure 7-2.

Sales	
Eastern	$120,000
Western	60,000
Southern	144,000
	324,000

Figure 8-9

```
v ariable costs
    Production                                    199,800
    Marketing                                      22,680
                                              ──────────
    Total                                         222,480
                                              ──────────
Marginal income                                   101,520
                                              ──────────
Marginal income percentage                        .313333
Direct fixed costs
    Production                                     40,125
    Marketing                                       1,200
                                              ──────────
                                                   41,325
                                              ──────────
            Total product contribution        $  60,195
                                              ══════════
```

D. Revenue required to maintain the same product contribution
    1. Monthly marginal income required

Current product contribution	$ 60,195
Plant fixed costs	43,125
Marketing fixed costs	1,200
Total marginal income required	$104,520

    2. Marginal income percentage

Current product selling price	$120.00
Variable costs	
Production	64.00
Marketing (7% of sales)	8.40
Total cost	72.40
Marginal income	$ 47.60
Marginal income percentage	.396667

    3. Sales volume required:

$$\frac{\text{required marginal income}}{\text{marginal income percentage}} = \frac{\$104,520}{.396667} = \$263,496$$

Figure 8-9 (Continued)

for monthly administrative costs of $25,000) of operating plant 1 of the Hypothetical Corporation, which produces only product Red. The cost data are summarized in Figure 8-9. Because plant 1 produces only product Red, all costs of the plant are directly traceable to this product. Hence any change in the cost structure of the plant can be evaluated in terms of its impact on product Red contribution.

The proposed cost change comes about in this example because of a suggestion that automated machines be installed in the grinding department. This automatic machinery will reduce labor cost by $10 for each unit produced, but monthly fixed expenses of the plant will increase by $3,000; the new unit cost will be $64, and the total plant monthly fixed expenses will be $43,125. Current planned monthly contribution for product Red is $60,195, and one of the questions facing the decision maker is: what dollar sales volume must be generated with the new cost structure to produce the same contribution?

The required monthly marginal income is computed by summing direct fixed costs and the total product contribution currently planned for the month. This amount is divided by the new marginal income ratio for product Red of .396667 to arrive at a sales amount of $263,496. Since the current plan is for monthly sales of $324,000, sales can fall by $60,504 before the currently planned product contribution is imperiled. Moreover, because the marginal income percentage after the cost change (.396667) is higher than the former (.313333), increases in sales above $263,496 will be more profitable with the new cost structure than with the old. On the other hand, if future sales of product Red are uncertain, with a strong possibility of a sales decline, the existing cost structure is preferable because of the low monthly fixed costs.

REFERENCES

1. Devine, Carl T., "Boundaries and Potentials of Reporting on Profit-Volume Relationships, "*Management Accounting* (formerly *NAA Bulletin*) (January 1961), pp. 5–14.

2. Ferrara, William L., "Breakeven for Individual Products, Plants, and Sales Territories," *Management Advisor* (formerly *Management Services*) (July–August 1964), pp. 38–47.

3. National Association of Accountants, *The Analysis of Cost-Volume-Profit Relationships*, Research Reports 16, 17, and 18 New York: National Association of Accountants, 1950.

CHAPTER 9

CONTRIBUTION ANALYSIS

Chapter 8 was devoted to a discussion of how direct cost information is used in cost–volume–profit analyses to provide relevant data for various types of planning decisions. The discussion is expanded in this chapter to include a number of additional planning decisions. For instance, the sell-or-process-further decision, the make-or-buy decision, and the product mix decision are reviewed here to illustrate how direct cost and contribution data can be utilized as information inputs to such decisions. The use of contribution data for segment profitability analysis, product mix decisions, and salesmen compensation plans is also discussed.

However, before examining any of these specific decision types in detail, the decision framework in which such decisions are made is reviewed. As mentioned in Chapter 1, planning decisions can be made at several levels in the organization, and three levels were noted in that chapter: strategic planning, management control, and operational control. The top two levels—strategic planning and management control—are involved in varying degrees with the decisions covered in this chapter. For example, the conditions under which sell-or-process-further decisions can be made are usually established at the strategic planning decision level, and the implementation of these guidelines is commonly achieved by decisions at the management control level.

It is important for policies to be established at the strategic planning level because of the broader perspective of the decision makers who make these decisions. The possible impact on customers and suppliers in both the short and the long run must be evaluated before the short-run economics of the decision are considered. Once a decision has been made at the strategic planning level to consider a make-or-buy question, for example, and policies and profit guides have been established, the implementation of these policies is ordinarily carried out at the management control level. It is at this decision level that direct cost and contribution data are most useful. These data do receive consideration by the managers making the strategic planning decision, but they play a far more significant role at the management control level because of the tendency for such decisions to be concerned with short-run phenomena. Because direct cost and contribution data contribute to the economic evaluation aspects of these decisions, the remainder of this chapter assumes that policies setting forth the conditions under which these decisions can be made have already been established.

MAKE–OR–BUY DECISIONS

In evaluating the economic consequences of the make-or-buy decision, the decision maker compares the expected cost of producing a product with the

Summary of Manufacturing Costs from Figure 5-3

Machining			
Material		$ 8.00	
Labor		10.00	
Overhead		4.00	$22.00
		_____	
Overhead budget:			
Rate per machine hour	$.50		
Amount	$1,500		
Grinding			
Material		$ 1.50	
Labor		12.00	
Overhead		3.00	16.50
		_____	
Overhead budget:			
Rate per labor hour	$1.00		
Amount	$1,200		
Assembly			
Material		$12.00	
Labor		15.00	
Overhead		8.50	35.50
		_____	_____
Overhead budget:			
Rate per labor hour	$1.70		
Amount	$1,325		
Total product cost			$74.00

Figure 9-1

Economic Analysis for Make-or-Buy Decision: Buy and Eliminate Facilities

---

Offer by outside supplier: Each month 1,000 units will be supplied at a price of $80 apiece.

Cost analysis of offer		
Cost of outside purchase		$80,000
Direct variable costs (Figure 9-1)		$74,000
Direct monthly fixed costs (Figure 9-1)		
Machining	$1,500	
Grinding	1,200	
Assembly	1,325	4,025
Total cost of making		$78,025
Cost increase because of outside purchase		$ 1,975

Figure 9-2

expected cost of buying the product. As an illustration consider the production cost data first presented in Figure 5-3 and summarized here in Figure 9-1. These data contain the direct fixed and variable costs of producing a unit of product (assuming that only one product is manufactured by these three departments).

An analysis of a make-or-buy decision using these data is illustrated in Figure 9-2. In this case an outside supplier has offered to manufacture the product at a unit price of $80, which is $6 higher than the direct unit variable cost of producing the product. It appears that the company should reject the offer. However, in examining the economics of the decision, the manager must also consider the fixed costs that can be eliminated if the outside offer is accepted. These fixed costs and the variable production costs are combined to arrive at the total cost that can be eliminated if the offer from the outside supplier is accepted. By eliminating all the costs directly related to producing the product in this case, the company will reduce its monthly costs by $78,025, which will be offset by an increase in purchases of $80,000. The net result—a monthly cost increase of $1,975—indicates that the offer should not be accepted. Thus, even if the fixed costs to be eliminated are included in the analysis, it is clear that the company will have higher profits if it rejects the offer instead of accepting it.

Notice that this example is based on the assumption that the direct fixed costs of producing the product are to be eliminated if the outside offer is accepted. If the costs will continue even though the offer from the outside supplier is accepted, the analysis must be expanded to consider the effect on the company profits of maintaining the facilities. In other words, the make-or-buy decision in this case evolves into a decision on how to best use the facilities the company has available.

For example, consider what the profit effect of accepting the offer will be if the facilities that are currently being used to produce the product are shifted to the production of a new product. Data for this example are provided in Figure 9-3. In this instance the company pays $80,000 to buy the product from the outside supplier, thereby eliminating the $74,000 direct variable costs of production. Although this action results in a $6,000 increase in costs, this cost increase is more than offset by the additional marginal income generated by the new product that will be produced with the facilities formerly used to produce the product now being purchased. Consequently, the company is in a better profit position if it buys the product from an outside supplier, even though the price is higher than direct unit variable cost. In this case the decision maker generates the maximum profit for the company by paying an outside supplier more for a product than he would have to pay to produce it in his company because the plant facilities currently used to make the product can be used more profitably to produce another product. In make-or-buy decisions, then, the decision maker should consider not only the cost effect of the purchase from the outside supplier, he should also evaluate the potential marginal income available from alternative products that could be produced from the existing facilities.

Economic Analysis for Make-or-Buy Decision:
Buy and Use Facilities for Other Products

Cost of outside purchase (Figure 9-2)		$80,000
Variable cost eliminated		74,000
Net cost increase		$ 6,000
Revenue from new product: 2,000 units @$75	$150,000	
Variable cost of producing new product: 2,000 units @$60	120,000	
Marginal income from new product		30,000
Increase in profit from buying outside and producing new product		$24,000

Figure 9-3

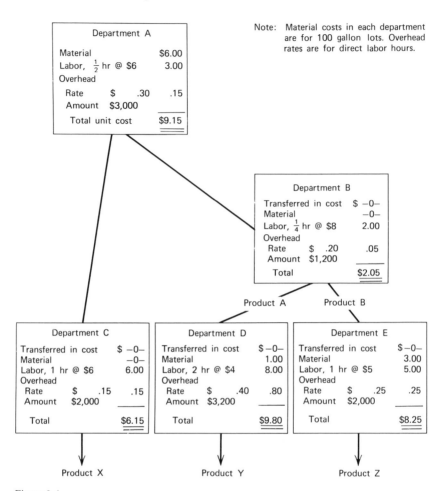

Figure 9-4

SELL–OR–PROCESS–FURTHER DECISIONS

Another decision for which direct cost and contribution data are relevant is the sell-or-process-further decision, which must be made when a raw material passes through several departments, the output of each department through which it passes being salable as a finished product or usable as an input to another department. The choice, then, is between selling a specific department's output or processing it through another department. The decision maker considers both the revenue that can be received from selling the product at an early point in the production process and the marginal income that can be earned after additional processing. Direct cost data that have already been assembled for product costs can be used to develop the data needed for this decision.

Consider, for instance, the product cost data originally illustrated in Figure 5-6, reproduced here in Figure 9-4. Assume that the output of department B that consists of product B can either be sold as a finished product or processed through department E and afterward sold. The analysis for this decision appears in Figure 9-5: the decision maker can sell the output of department B as product B for a price of $100 for 100 gallons, or he can process product B in department E and sell the resulting output at a price of $105 for 100 gallons. In the example in Figure 9-5 the decision maker has 10,000 gallons of product B that can be processed or sold. If he sells product B, he will have $10,000 of revenue; but if he processes it through the last department and sells it as product Z, his marginal income will be $11,610. This analysis indicates that the product should be processed through the last department because such added processing results in the greatest profit for the company.

Economic Analysis for Sell-or-Process: Further Decision

Revenue data	
Current selling price, product A (100 gallons)	$ 100
Current selling price, product Z (100 gallons)	$ 105
(Note: 100 gallons of product A will produce 120 gallons of product Z.)	
Analysis of decision for 10,000 gallons of product B	
Current revenue	$10,000
Revenue from product Z (12,000 gallons)	$12,600
Department E cost of processing (12,000 × 8.25/100)	990
Marginal income	$11,610
Alternate form of analysis	
Increase in revenue ($12,600 − $10,000)	$ 2,600
Increase in cost	990
Increase in marginal income	$ 1,610

Figure 9-5

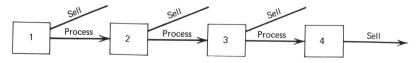

Figure 9.6*a* Multistage analysis of sell-or-process-further decision.

Numerical Illustration of Multistage Decision

I. Data for illustration
    Revenue available at end of each process
    Process 1 $ 8,000
    Process 2   8,500
    Process 3   12,000
    Process 4   14,000
    Cost of processing product through each process:
    Process 1   irrelevant for this analysis
    Process 2 $ 1,000
    Process 3   1,000
    Process 4   4,500

II. Multistage analysis
    A. Sell at end of process 1 or process 2

Revenue, process 1		$ 8,000
Process 2		
Revenue	$ 8,500	
Added cost	1,000	7,500
Excess of process 1 revenue over process 2 marginal income		$ 500

    B. Sell at end of process 1 or process 3

Revenue, process 1		$ 8,000
Revenue, process 3	$12,000	
Costs		
Process 2	1,000	
Process 3	1,000	
Total	2,000	10,000
Excess of process 3 marginal income over process 1 revenue		$ 2,000

    C. Sell at end of process 1 or process 4

Revenue, process 1		$ 8,000
Revenue, process 4	$14,000	

Costs		
Process 2	1,000	
Process 3	1,000	
Process 4	4,500	
Total	6,500	7,500
Excess of process 1 revenue over process 4 marginal income	$ 500	

Figure 9.6*b*

An alternate form of analysis consists of comparing the added sales revenue from additional processing with the added cost of additional processing. If the additional revenue exceeds the additional cost, the product should be processed. In this example, the additional revenue is $2,600 and the additional cost is $990; thus the analysis indicates that further processing is the more profitable alternative. If the added cost exceeds the added revenue, the analysis indicates that the product should be sold without any added processing.

Although the example in Figure 9-5 shows a comparison of the revenue from selling department B output with the marginal income from additional processing through department E, the decision is seldom so simple. Frequently the output of a department flows through several succeeding production processes before arriving at finished goods, and the output of each process may be sold (see Figure 9-6a). A decision maker who is deciding whether to sell or process further at the end of process 1 must consider the profit impact of selling at the end of each succeeding process. He should not confine his analysis to a comparison of the results of selling at the end of the first two processes. If he does, he may find that his analysis indicates that the product should be sold at the end of process 1 because the increase in selling price from process 1 to process 2 is exceeded by the added cost of processing. However, including process 3 and process 4 in the analysis may indicate that the product should be processed through process 3 or even process 4 before being sold.

The data analysis of Figure 9-6b illustrates this multistage analysis of the decision. As the analysis reveals, the decision maker will decide to sell the output of process 1 instead of processing it further if he restricts his analysis to a comparison of the sale at the end of process 1 to the sale at the end of process 2. If he compares the sale at the end of process 1 with the marginal income from the sale of the product at the end of each succeeding process, as in Figure 9-6b, the decision maker will find that the product should be processed through process 3 before being sold. In preparing an analysis like this, the accountant should present data that indicate not only whether a product should be sold or processed further but also the point at which the product should be sold. For example, if the revenue available at the end of process 2 in Figure 9-6b had amounted to $9,500, the first analysis would have indicated further processing through process 2; but the analysis would not have indicated how much further to process the product. A multistage analysis, however, allows the decision maker to view the entire process from beginning to end; thus he can identify the optimum point for selling his product.

SEGMENT PROFITABILITY ANALYSIS

In addition to using direct cost and contribution data for special decisions such as make-or-buy and sell-or-process-further, the decision maker can use these data for evaluating the profitability of revenue generating segments of the business. The marketing reports developed in Chapter 7 provide one illustration of the use of contribution analysis with respect to segment profitability analysis; and another illustration appears in Figure 9-7. This example shows how segment contribution and marginal income data can be prepared for department store managers. Not only are the marginal income and the contribution amounts given for each department, these amounts are related to the square feet used to generate these amounts. For instance, Housewares sales of $30,000 is three times as large as the amount for Drugs ($10,000), but the contribution of $1.40 produced by each square foot of floor space in the drug department is close to the $1.53 generated by Housewares.

This example also illustrates the relative insignificance for performance evaluation of the marginal income percentage. For instance, the ratios for Housewares and Toys are the same at 32.3% yet Housewares produces almost twice as much contribution. This difference in performance is further emphasized when the Housewares contribution per square foot ($1.53) is compared with that for Toys ($.95). In addition, the marginal income ratios of Drugs (59%) and Jewelry (40%) are both higher than Housewares, but the total contribution from each of these departments is less than that for Housewares, both in total and on a square footage basis. Consequently, departmental performance should be evaluated on total departmental contribution and not on departmental marginal income ratios. The profitability of the business is determined by the amount of contribution produced by each department, not by the departmental percentage margin.

	Total	Department			
		Drugs	Jewelry	Housewares	Toys
Sales	$61,000	$10,000	$6,000	$30,000	$15.000
Variable costs					
Merchandise	37,000	4,000	3,000	20,000	10,000
Commissions	1,150	100	600	300	150
	38,150	4,100	3,600	20,300	10,150
Marginal income	$22,850	$ 5,900	$2,400	$ 9,700	$ 4,850
Marginal income %		59%	40%	32.3%	32.3%
Fixed costs					
Salaries	1,000	200	300	400	100
Advertising	270	100	50	100	20
	1,270	300	350	500	120
Department con- tribution	$21,580	$ 5,600	$2,050	$ 9,200	$ 4,730
Common fixed costs					
Rent, utilities, etc.	6,000				
Store manager salary	1,000				
Advertising	4,000				
	11,000				
Net profit before taxes	$10,580				
Departmental area (sq. ft)	17,000	4,000	2,000	6,000	5,000
Marginal income/ sq. ft		$1.48	$1.20	$1.61	$.97
Contribution/sq. ft		$1.40	$1.02	$1.53	$.95

Figure 9-7

135

The marginal income for each square foot of space devoted to a department can be used to furnish the store manager with a rough estimate of the change in marginal income generated by a department if the size of the department is changed. For example, shifting 1,000 sq. ft from Toys to Housewares will change the marginal income amounts produced by these departments. The store manager can estimate this change by first assuming that marginal income from Toys will decrease by $970 ($.97 × 1,000 sq. ft) and that marginal income from Housewares will increase by $1,610 ($1.61 × 1,000 sq. ft). He can modify these amounts by considering the various factors that will affect the sales of the two departments, but the current marginal income for each square foot provides a good starting point for his analysis.

Although the department store example emphasizes the use of contribution analysis for evaluating departmental performance, revenue segment analysis can also be applied to the evaluation of customer profitability. Consider the case of the two customers given in Figure 9-8. Customer A buys $50,000 monthly, whereas customer B buys only $15,000 each month; sales to customer A have a marginal income ratio of 50%, customer B sales produce a marginal income ratio of 40%, and monthly contribution from customer A is three times greater than for customer B.

At first glance, it appears that customer A is a far more profitable customer than is customer B. And he is if the company has excess production capacity and is willing to add more customers whenever it can. However, before a manager can decide which customer is the more profitable, he must look beyond the amounts used to compute the customer contribution. He must consider, for example, the production facilities committed to producing for each customer. The data at the bottom of Figure 9-8 indicate that five times more machine time is devoted to customer A than to customer B. If the machine is operated at only one-half its capacity, this information is not too important; but as the usage of the machine approaches full capacity, this information becomes more critical to the decision maker. Consider, as an illustration, the situation of the sales manager who must decide what kinds of customers to solicit. When the machine is operating at one-half capacity, he will accept all types of customers. However, as production on the machine increases to near capacity, he will try to get more customers like customer B and fewer like customer A, because customer B sales generate $6 of marginal income for each machine hour, whereas customer A sales generate only $5 for each machine hour. When the machine is operating at full capacity, the company can increase its profits by replacing buyers like customer A with buyers like customer B.

In other words, the company will maximize its profits if it maximizes the marginal income for each machine hour. In this instance, then, customer profitability can be evaluated by a review of the marginal income the customer contributes for each machine hour devoted to him. Customer B is the more profitable customer in Figure 9-8 because he has a marginal income of $6 for each machine hour, as compared with $5 for customer A. In summary, company profits are maximized when the marginal income for each unit of the constraining factor is maximized. This holds true for customers as well as for individual products.

PRODUCT MIX DECISION

When using the concept of marginal income maximization per unit of the constraining factor, the accountant can perform a simple analysis like the one in Figure 9-8 if there is only one constraint. However, the analysis becomes more involved if there are several constraints to be considered, especially when there are several products that can be produced in varying amounts. Consider, for example, the two products in Figure 9-9—both are processed through the same machines in the fabricating and finishing departments. If production capacity is much greater than the number of units the market can absorb, the company will get the greatest possible marginal

Monthly Analysis of Customer Profitability

	Customer A	Customer B
Sales	$50,000	$15,000
Variable costs	25,000	9,000
Marginal income	$25,000	$ 6,000
Marginal income percentage	50%	40%
Direct fixed costs	10,000	1,000
Contribution to common costs	$15,000	$ 5,000
Contribution percentage	30%	33%
Machine hours devoted to producing for each customer	5,000	1,000
Marginal income per machine hour	$5	$6

Figure 9-8

Marginal Income Maximization: Two Products, Three Constraints

I. Product standards	Alpha	Beta
Sales price	$ 20	$ 30
Direct cost	7	15
Marginal income	$ 13	$ 15
Marginal income ratio	65%	50%
Machine hours		
Fabricating	4	6
Finishing	4	4

II. Production constraints

Fabricating machine hours available	120	
Finishing machine hours available	100	
Because of a shortage of storage space, no more than 20 units of Alpha can be produced during the production period.		

Figure 9-9

income by pushing the sales of product Beta. However, if everything that can be produced can be sold, the company must consider the factors constraining production. These factors are outlined in the second part of Figure 9-9.

The company maximizes its marginal income in this example by producing the maximum number of units permitted by the constraints, and by producing these units in a mix that causes the greatest marginal income to be generated. The company will not maximize its marginal income by producing all of one product and none of the other. For instance, the company can produce 20 units of product Beta and no units of Alpha for a total marginal income of $300; or it can produce 20 units of Alpha and no units of Beta for a marginal income of $200. Obviously, the company is in better financial condition if it produces all Beta and no Alpha. But it may be in an even better position if it produces some of each, and the linear programming model provides a powerful tool for determining how many units of each product the company should plan to produce to maximize marginal income.

A graphical illustration of the linear programming solution to the product mix decision is presented in Figure 9-10. The units of Beta appear on the horizontal axis, and the units of Alpha are on the vertical axis. The lines on the graph represent the production constraints mentioned in the second part of Figure 9-9. The line labeled "Finishing constraint" represents the various combinations of the two products that can be produced in the finishing department. For instance, if the 100 machine hours in the finishing department are used to produce only Alpha, 25 units of product will result; if the 100 hours are used to produce Beta, 25 units of this product can be produced. The line that is drawn from the 25 units of Alpha to the 25 units of Beta represents all possible combinations of the two products that can be produced in the finishing department. A line is

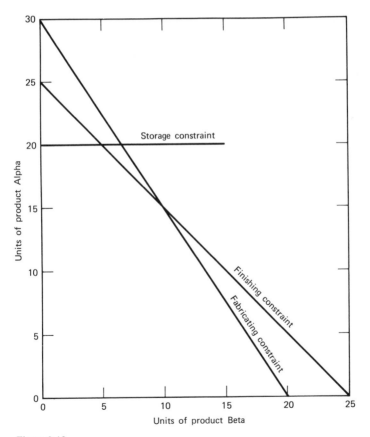

Figure 9-10

Product Mix Computation

Trial	Corner	Product Mix		Marginal Income		
		Beta	Alpha	Beta	Alpha	Total
1	0, 0	0	0	15(0) +	13(0) =	$-0-
2	20, 0	20	0	15(20) +	13(0) =	300
3	10, 15	10	15	15(10) +	13(15) =	345
4	5, 20	5	20	15(5) +	13(20) =	335
5	0, 20	0	20	15(0) +	13(20) =	260

Figure 9-11

drawn in the same way for the fabricating department. The horizontal line on the graph labeled "Storage constraint" indicates that no more than 20 units of Alpha can be produced during the production run because of storage limitations.

The area that is bounded by these straight lines represents the possible combinations of product that can be produced. For example, the maximum units of Alpha that can be produced is limited to 20 by the storage constraint, even though the productive capacity is available to produce more. Likewise, no more than 20 units of Beta can be produced, because 20 is the maximum number of units that can be handled by the fabricating department.

Because of the manner in which the linear programming model works, the optimum product mix is always at one of the corners of the area boxed in by the straight lines. The marginal income for each of these corners is summarized in Figure 9-11, which shows the amount of marginal income for each corner of the boxed-in area, starting with zero output of both units. By computing the marginal income amount at each corner, the accountant is able to identify the product mix that maximizes total marginal income. In this example, 15 units of Alpha and 10 units of Beta produce the maximum marginal income that can be derived from the production facilities available for manufacturing these two products. Shifting production away from this corner will result in less marginal income because the marginal income per unit of constraining factor will not be maximized. Consider, for example, the effect on marginal income of a shift from corner (10, 15). If production is shifted from this corner to corner (5, 20), one unit of Alpha can be produced for each unit of Beta given up. This means that each 4 hours of machine time in the finishing department that had been generating $15 of marginal income can now generate only $13 of marginal income. Consequently, such a change in the product mix will result in less than the maximum marginal income per unit of the constraining factor.

The same thing happens if the production is shifted toward corner (20, 0). As product mix shifts in this direction, the limiting factor is the number of hours available in the fabricating department; and 1.5 units of Alpha must be given up to release enough machine time to produce a single unit of Beta. The marginal income given up is $19.50, and this is replaced by only $15.00 of marginal income. Hence shifting production in the direction of corner (20, 0) does not maximize the marginal income per unit of the constraining factor. The only point at which the marginal income per unit of constraining factor is maximized is at corner (10, 15).

Notice that this analysis made no mention of the marginal income ratios. This factor was neglected because marginal income is not maximized by pushing the product with the highest ratio unless there is excess productive capacity.

The example just used is extremely simple; however, the principle of maximizing marginal income per unit of constraining factor holds true even for problems with 400 products and 200 constraints. Regardless of the size of the linear programming problem, costs must be separated into their fixed and variable components before the data can be used to determine the product mix. In a direct cost system the cost data are already separated; thus additional cost analysis is seldom needed to prepare the data for the linear programming model.

SALESMAN COMPENSATION PLANS

The use of contribution analysis for evaluating revenue segments was discussed earlier in this chapter to show how such an analysis could serve in the evaluation of the adequacy of segment contribution. The same type of analysis can be employed to examine the economic rationale of salesman compensation plans.

Consider the case of the two Western Territory salesmen in Figure 9–12: both receive 4% of gross sales as their compensation for selling the three products produced by this company. The data at the top of the figure show that the marginal income ratios vary from 75% for product A to 30% for product C. Salesman Jones generated $100,000 of sales in July, but salesman Smith sold only $70,000; nevertheless, the marginal income produced by both salesmen is the same at $40,500. Furthermore, salesman Jones incurred $5,000 in expenses, as compared with only $1,500 for Smith.

I. Total sales of Western Territory for July

	Total	Product A	B	C
Sales	$170,000	$40,000	$60,000	$70,000
Variable costs	89,000	10,000	30,000	49,000
Marginal income	$ 81,000	$30,000	$30,000	$21,000
Marginal income percentage	47.6%	75%	50%	30%

II. Salesman R. Jones

	Total	A	B	C
Sales	$100,000	$10,000	$30,000	$60,000
Variable costs	59,500	2,500	15,000	42,000
Marginal income	$ 40,500	$ 7,500	$15,000	$18,000

Expenses	
Travel and entertainment	2,000
Rush order costs	3,000
Total	5,000
Contribution before commissions	35,500
Commissions (4% of sales)	4,000
Contribution	$ 31,500

III. Salesman J. Smith

	Total	A	B	C
Sales	$ 70,000	$30,000	$30,000	$10,000
Variable costs	29,500	7,500	15,000	7,000
Marginal income	$ 40,500	$22,500	$15,000	$ 3,000

Expenses	
Travel and entertainment	1,000
Rush order costs	500
Total	1,500
Contribution before commissions	39,000
Commissions (4% of sales)	2,800
Contribution	$ 36,200

Figure 9-12

As a result, Jones has a contribution of $35,500 before his commissions are deducted, whereas Smith has a contribution of $39,000.

Smith also contributes more to company profits than does Jones, but look who gets the bigger paycheck. Not Smith; his sales were 30% less than those of Jones. This compensation plan, because of its fixation on the sales figure, has rewarded the salesman who attempted to maximize his earnings and penalized the salesman who attempted to maximize company profits. In other words, the salesman gets no immediate compensation for trying to help the company maximize its profits.

A more reasonable compensation plan (see Figure 9–13) is based on salesman contribution to company profits; this means that the greater the contribution a salesman makes to company profits, the greater his immediate reward. Such a compensation plan links the amount of compensation a salesman earns to the degree to which he helps the company meet its profit goal. No longer will a salesman be able to increase his earnings by pushing easy-to-sell, low-margin items or by cutting prices to increase his sales. Any decision he makes that causes his contribution to decline will also cause his compensation to decline. The data in Figure 9-13 reveal that under a compensation plan based on a fixed percentage of contribution, Smith has greater earnings than Jones. The same is true when a sliding scale of percentages is used.

Another advantage of this form of compensation plan is that the salesman influences his earnings by controlling his costs and managing his selling performance. If a salesman can increase his contribution by increasing the amount he spends on entertainment, it is to his advantage to do so. If the salesman becomes wasteful in the way he spends money on

Salesman Compensation Plans

I. Plan based on fixed percentage of contribution

	Jones	Smith
Contribution before commissions	$35,500	$39,000
Commissions (8% of contribution)	2,840	3,120
Salesman contribution to common costs and profit	$32,660	$35,880

II. Plan based on sliding scale commissions

Commission Rate Schedule

Contribution	Rate (%)
0–20,000	3
20,000–25,000	5
25,000–30,000	10
30,000–35,000	15
above 35,000	20

	Jones	Smith
Contribution before commissions	$35,500	$39,000
Commissions		
0–20,000	600	600
20,000–25,000	250	250
25,000–30,000	500	500
30,000–35,000	750	750
above 35,000	100	800
Total	2,200	2,900
Contribution to common costs and profit	$33,000	$36,100

Figure 9-13

entertaining customers, his earnings decrease. Consequently, a compensation plan based on contribution rewards the salesman for wisely managing his expenditures and his selling effort. This compensation plan makes the profit goal of the salesman coincide with the profit goal of the company.

CHAPTER 10

DIRECT COSTS
FOR PRICING DECISIONS

Pricing decisions are not simple decisions, and direct costs do not provide simple answers to complex pricing decisions. However, pricing managers can make better pricing decisions with direct cost data than with absorption cost data, and this chapter focuses on situations in which direct cost information is helpful to pricing decisions. No attempt is made to provide a methodology for considering all the factors that affect the price of a product. The references for this chapter include several books and articles that discuss numerous facets of pricing decisions, and the reader who is interested in exploring this topic in greater detail can refer to these publications.

This chapter begins with a discussion of the economics of pricing, aimed at providing the underlying rationale for the remainder of the chapter. We explore the concepts of demand and supply in terms of their impact on prices; price elasticity of demand is also examined. Then we deal with the different ways in which contribution data can be used in setting prices; finally, the pricing of special offers is reviewed to illustrate how direct cost data are useful for these decisions.

ECONOMICS OF PRICING*

The pricing mechanism is used in most free enterprise economic systems as a tool for channeling available resources into those uses which will provide the products that consumers want most. If an insufficient quantity of a

---

* Richard H. Leftwich, *The Price System and Resource Allocation,* 3rd ed. (New York: Holt, Rinehart, Winston, 1966), contains a clear, readable presentation of the economic theory of pricing.

145

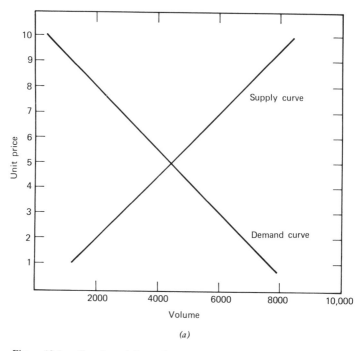

(a)

Figure 10-1a   Supply and demand curves.

Demand Schedule		Supply Schedule	
Market Price	Units Demanded	Market Price	Units Supplied
1	7,600	1	1,200
2	6,800	2	2,000
3	6,000	3	2,800
4	5,200	4	3,600
5	4,400	5	4,400
6	3,600	6	5,200
7	2,800	7	6,000
8	2,000	8	6,800
9	1,200	9	7,600
10	400	10	8,400

Figure 10-1b

given product is being produced, customers bid up the price of the product that is available; and this increased price makes it profitable for more firms to produce the product, until enough units are produced to satisfy customers. Conversely, as customers want less of a product, the price they will pay for the units of that product drops. This lower price causes fewer firms to produce the product until the quantity of the product produced declines to a level that just satisfies the number of customers who want the product.

The market price for a product is established at the point at which the demand curve for the product and the supply curve for the product intersect. Figure 10-1 *a*, shows a graph depicting this relationship. The demand curve represents the various volumes of goods that customers are willing to buy at the various product prices; the supply curve represents the various quantities that firms are willing to produce at the various product prices. These data appear in Figure 10-1*b*. As the numbers show, the quantities of product that customers are willing to buy equals the quantities that firms are willing to produce at a market price of $5. If the demand curve shifts to the right (an indication that the market demand for the product has increased), the market price will increase; this increased price will then cause more firms to offer the product because of the higher price. Shifts to the left in the demand curve cause firms to take the opposite actions. Similarly, the supply curve can be moved back and forth to demonstrate the effect on price of changes in the total supply of the product.

As the data in the demand schedule show, customers are willing to buy a greater volume of a product as the price of that product goes down, and the opposite is true for price increases. The relationship of the change in sales volume to the change in price is called the *elasticity of demand*. The greater the volume change in relation to the price change, the greater the elasticity of demand. For instance, if a price increase of 10% results in a 90% reduction in volume, the demand for that product is highly elastic. On the other hand, if a 10% price increase on another product causes no change in the volume sold, the demand for that product is inelastic. Because it measures the effect on sales volume of a change in price, knowledge of the elasticity of demand for a product is important for effective pricing decisions.

The supply curve for a given market is influenced by the cost structures of the firms serving that market. The theoretical unit cost curves for a firm are presented in Figure 10-2. The graph in this figure depicts several unit cost curves.

1. *Average fixed cost.* This curve slopes downward to the right because the fixed cost per unit of output decreases as the units produced increases.

2. *Average variable cost.* The average variable cost curve has a "U"

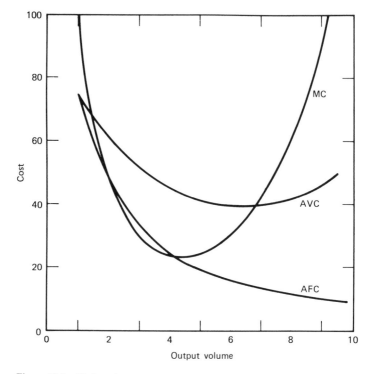

Figure 10-2   Unit cost curves.

shape because variable costs per unit are high at low levels of production due to the inefficiencies that are present when the plant is operating below its designed level. At high levels of production this unit cost rises because of the law of diminishing returns; simply stated, this means that as the maximum capacity of the plant is approached, increases in production volume require ever higher increases in variable cost.

3. *Marginal cost.* This curve represents the added cost of producing one more unit of product. It assumes a "U" shape for the same reason as the average variable cost; however, it is a leading indicator of the average variable cost, always increasing or decreasing ahead of increases or decreases in average variable cost.

The numbers from which these cost curves are derived are listed in Figure 10-3. The cost curves can be used to demonstrate how the market price for a product affects the supply of that product; in other words, the curves show how a firm decides on the number of units of a given product it is willing to produce at a given price. If the output that a firm is willing to produce for each of several different market prices is listed in a table, that table will indicate the various supply amounts that correspond to the different market prices. That is, the table shows a supply curve.

The cost that the firm considers in deciding how many units to produce is the marginal cost of the units of product; all other costs are irrelevant to the pricing decision. In deciding how many units to produce, the firm will choose the quantity of units that causes marginal cost to equal marginal revenue. This means that production will be increased until the marginal cost rises to the point at which it is equal to marginal revenue.

Marginal revenue is defined as the added revenue generated from the sale of one more unit of product. Since the revenue generated from the sale of a unit of product varies with the price of the product, at high prices the firm will increase its output, and at low prices it will decrease its output. And because the price of the product sold by the firm is determined by the demand curve facing the firm, the firm will charge the price that causes customers to demand an output volume that makes marginal cost equal marginal revenue.

Figure 10-4 is a numerical example of this relationship between marginal revenue and marginal cost; the data were developed for the same firm for which cost data were illustrated in Figure 10-3. The marginal revenue column is derived by computing the increase in total sales revenue from selling

Illustration of cost relationships

Quantity	Total Fixed Costs	Average Fixed Costs	Total Variable Costs	Average Variable Costs	Total Costs	Marginal Costs
0	100	—	0	—	100	—
1	100	100	75	75	175	75
2	100	50	125	63	225	50
3	100	33	155	52	255	30
4	100	25	180	45	280	25
5	100	20	205	41	305	25
6	100	17	240	40	340	35
7	100	15	290	41	390	50
8	100	13	355	44	455	65
9	100	11	450	50	550	95
10	100	10	585	59	685	135

Figure 10-3

Cost and Revenue Relationships

Price	Units Demanded	Dollar Sales	Marginal Revenue	Marginal Costs	Total Costs	Profit
$160	1	$160	$160	$ 75	$175	$(15)
150	2	300	140	50	225	75
140	3	420	120	30	255	165
130	4	520	100	25	280	240
120	5	600	80	25	305	295
110	6	660	60	35	340	320
100	7	700	40	50	390	310
90	8	720	20	65	455	265
80	9	720	0	95	550	170
70	10	700	− 20	135	685	15

Figure 10-4

one more unit. Since price must be lowered to increase units sold, the total revenue derived from the new price and the quantity sold must be compared with the former total revenue, to arrive at the marginal revenue amount.

The marginal costs and total costs from Figure 10-3 have been added to the revenue data in Figure 10-4; thus the total profit can be computed for the firm at the various price levels. These data indicate that the firm can maximize its profits by producing between 6 and 7 units of product. At that production level the marginal cost and the marginal revenue are equal, and the company earns the greatest possible profit. Because of the simplicity of this example, the marginal costs and marginal revenue are not equal at the maximum profit of $320. However, if fractional units and finer product price gradations are used, the profits will be maximized at the point at which marginal revenue equals marginal cost.

This discussion of the economic theory of pricing is of necessity brief; yet the pricing manager can use these ideas even if he cannot apply them in the manner in which they were discussed here. For example, the standard direct unit cost of a product as it has been treated previously is a close approximation of the marginal cost as discussed in this chapter. Of course this approximation holds true only for the normal range of production. Consequently, if a company can increase its sales by reducing its prices, it should reduce prices until its marginal revenue equals its direct unit cost. Although instances in which a company can accurately predict the change in sales resulting from a change in prices are rare, this pricing approach is sometimes relevant. However, the pricing manager must always keep in mind that profits are maximized when marginal revenue equals marginal cost only when price reductions cause increases in the volume of goods sold.

In such cases, if the company is operating at normal capacity, the direct standard unit cost can be used as a surrogate for marginal cost. If the company is operating above normal capacity, an amount in excess of standard direct cost should be used because the standard cost usually reflects the unit cost of operating within the normal range of activity. At production levels in excess of normal capacity, the marginal costs increase faster than increases in output. And because the marginal cost is a leading indicator of unit variable cost, these cost increases will usually be reflected in the accounting records several months after they have taken place.

Before attempting to set a price that equals marginal cost, the pricing manager must also deal with the practical considerations that price reductions do not necessarily increase sales in all cases, and price increases do not necessarily reduce sales in all cases. For instance, customers may interpret a price reduction in one of the following ways:*

1. The product is to be superseded by a later model.
2. Customers do not like the item, and the company is cutting prices to unload its excess stock.
3. The item is no longer in season.
4. The company is in financial trouble and is trying to raise cash. Consequently, it may not be in business long enough to honor warranties and so on.

If a customer places any one of these interpretations on the price reduction, it will offset the attractiveness of the lowered product price.

The same type of problem is encountered in predicting the reaction of customers to a price increase. Not every customer will buy less of a product because its price is increased, as the following possible interpretations of a price increase illustrate:†

1. There is a limited supply of the item available, and if it is not bought soon, it will be unobtainable.
2. The item is the most desirable style available.
3. The item is an excellent product, and the seller could not make a profit at the old price.

* Alfred R. Oxenfeldt, *Pricing for Marketing Executives* (Belmont, Calif.: Wadsworth, 1961), p. 28.
† Ibid.

Consequently, the pricing manager should carefully analyze his product and the market at which it is being aimed before he draws conclusions about the effect on sales volume of a change in selling price.

When the quantity sold does vary inversely with the price charged, the pricing manager should know something about the elasticity of demand for his product. As a practical matter, the elasticity of demand cannot be accurately computed for a specific product; but a general knowledge of the elasticity of demand for a product is important to rational pricing decisions, even though a precise measure for elasticity is not available. In other words, the concept of elasticity of demand is valuable to pricing decisions even though measurements of elasticity, from a practical viewpoint, are very difficult to develop.

CONTRIBUTION APPROACH TO PRICING*

This section expands some of the concepts mentioned in the previous section by illustrating how contribution analysis can be used to make pricing decisions. Both the use of contribution targets for revenue generating segments and the use of contribution analysis for special deals are explored to demonstrate how contribution analysis can be used to make pricing decisions.

Contribution targets for sales territories can be used in establishing selling prices by setting a minimum amount that a territory should contribute to common costs and company profits. The territory target contribution amount is developed by considering the amount of advertising that will influence territory sales, the number of salesmen working in the territory, and the actions competitors are likely to take during the planning period. A company can evaluate the effect of changes in promotion expenditures by using the type of analysis illustrated in Figure 10-5, which lists the respective contributions from three products for various levels of promotion expenditure. Product contribution is shown for the three products at the current level of promotion expenditure in the first section of this figure, and the results of increasing and decreasing these expenditures for each of the products are presented in the second two sections.

This format allows the marketing managers to focus on the impact on contribution of changes in promotion expenditure. For instance, increasing promotion costs increases product contribution for all products except product B. On the other hand, decreasing promotion expenditures from the

* National Association of Accountants, *Product Costs for Pricing Purposes,* Research Report 24. (New York:National Association of Accountants, 1953). Chapter 7 contains an excellent discussion of the various ways in which contribution data can be used for pricing decisions.

current level results in an increase in product contribution for product B in excess of the amount generated from the current level of promotion cost.

Another form of analysis that is developed when setting segment contribution targets is the price–volume analysis illustrated in Figure 10-6. This analysis may be performed after the promotion expenditure analysis, or it may be performed jointly with the promotion expenditure analysis.

Segment Contribution Targets: Promotion Expenditure Analysis

I. Product contribution prior to change in promotion expenditures

| | | | Product | |
	Total	A	B	C
Sales	$120,000	$50,000	$30,000	$40,000
Variable costs	61,000	30,000	15,000	16,000
Marginal income	59,000	20,000	15,000	24,000
Promotion expenditures	21,000	10,000	5,000	6,000
Contribution	$ 38,000	$10,000	$10,000	$18,000

II. Promotion costs increased $2,000 for each product

	Total	A	B	C
Sales	$138,000	$60,000	$33,000	$45,000
Variable costs	70,500	36,000	16,500	18,000
Marginal income	67,500	24,000	16,500	27,000
Promotion expenditures	27,000	12,000	7,000	8,000
Contribution	$ 40,500	$12,000	$ 9,500	$19,000

III. Promotion costs decreased $2,000 for each product

	Total	A	B	C
Sales	$103,000	$40,000	$28,000	$35,000
Variable costs	52,000	24,000	14,000	14,000
Marginal income	51,000	16,000	14,000	21,000
Promotion expenditures	15,000	8,000	3,000	4,000
Contribution	$ 36,000	$ 8,000	$11,000	$17,000

Figure 10-5

Segment Contribution Targets: Price–Volume Analysis

I. Product contribution prior to price change

	Total	Product A	B	C
Sales	$120,000	$50,000	$30,000	$40,000
Variable costs	61,000	30,000	15,000	16,000
Marginal income	59,000	20,000	15,000	24,000
Fixed costs	21,000	10,000	5,000	6,000
Contribution	$ 38,000	$10,000	$10,000	$18,000

II. Product contribution with 10% price decrease

	Total	A	B	C
Sales	$155,000	$75,000	$35,000	$45,000
Variable costs	89,050	50,000	19,250	19,800
Marginal income	65,950	25,000	15,750	25,200
Fixed costs	21,000	10,000	5,000	6,000
Contribution	$ 44,950	$15,000	$10,750	$19,200

III. Product contribution with 10% price increase

	Total	A	B	C
Sales	$ 98,000	$30,000	$30,000	$38,000
Variable costs	43,220	16,800	13,500	12,920
Marginal income	54,780	13,200	16,500	25,080
Fixed costs	21,000	10,000	5,000	6,000
Contribution	$ 33,780	$ 3,200	$11,500	$19,080

Figure 10-6

Price–volume analysis looks at the effect of price changes on the volume of products sold in a revenue generating segment to determine what level of segment contribution should be established as a target. The analysis can also be used to evaluate the chances of obtaining a pre-established segment contribution target. In the example in Figure 10-6, the effect on product contribution of price increases and price decreases is presented to reveal what estimated contribution looks like for various combinations of selling prices and sales volumes. The data in Figure 10-6 indicate that the demand for product A is highly elastic, since a 10% price reduction results in a $5,000 increase in product contribution. Product B benefits very little from the price reduction, but product C generates $1,200 more product contribution as a result of the price reduction. Price increases, on the other hand, cause a reduction in product contribution for product A; but product B shows an increase in product contribution of $1500 over the current level. Product C contribution for the price increase is only slightly less than the contribution amount estimated for the 10% price decrease. After reviewing this price–volume analysis, company managers can decide how much the target contribution amount should be for the various revenue generating segments.

Target contribution amounts and product prices can also be developed by following a procedure that starts with a desired before-tax return on investment. This rate is used to compute desired before-tax profit for the company; in turn, this profit amount is used to compute the total contribution amount required to produce this profit. Finally, the target contribution amounts for the various segments are split off from the total desired contribution, and product prices are computed.

This process is illustrated in Figure 10-7 for a company with three sales territories. The same form of analysis can be used for products, product lines, or for company divisions; in all cases, the analysis starts with a desired profit or contribution. In the example given, the company desires a 20% return on assets before taxes, and it has total assets of $5 million. Fixed costs common to the sales territories amount to $500,000, and direct fixed costs of the individual territories total $235,000. Planned unit sales for each territory for each product have been developed, and data on current selling prices and planned unit costs have also been assembled.

The target contribution computation appears in the second part of Figure 10-7. This amount consists of the target before-tax profit of $1 million plus the common fixed costs of $500,000. The total contribution desired is apportioned among the three sales territories in the amounts at the bottom of Figure 10-7. The relative amount of contribution assigned to a territory is a matter of judgment, and historical data on territory contribution, territory unit sales, unit selling prices, expected competitor activities, and numerous other factors are considered in making this decision. No standard formula can be used to compute the contribution amount that should be generated by a sales territory.

Figure 10-8 illustrates the next step in the process of arriving at unit prices. The contribution targets computed in Figure 10-7 and the territory direct fixed costs from the same figure are used to compute the target

I. Basic data
  A. Desired rate of return on assets before taxes   20%
  B. Total assets $5,000,000
  C. Annual fixed costs
  Direct fixed costs of administration and production $ 500,000
  Direct fixed costs of sales territories

Territory	Amount
East	$100,000
West	60,000
South	75,000
	$235,000

  D. Planned unit sales for each territory for the year

	Product	
Territory	A	B
East	40,000	30,000
West	20,000	10,000
South	15,000	15,000

  E. Current selling prices and expected unit costs
    1. Eastern Territory

	Product	
	A	B
Sales price	$18	$31
Standard cost	10	15
Marginal income	$ 8	$16

156

2. Western Territory

Sales price	$22	$32
Standard cost	10	15
Marginal income	$12	$17

3. Southern Territory

	Product	
	A	B
Sales price	$20	$30
Standard cost	10	15
Marginal income	$10	$15

II. Target contribution computation

Desired before-tax profit (20% × $5,000,000)	$1,000,000
Direct fixed costs of administration and production	500,000
Total contribution required from sales territories	$1,500,000

Contribution apportioned to sales territories:

Territory	Proportion (%)	Amount
East	50	$ 750,000
West	20	300,000
South	30	450,000
		$1,500,000

Figure 10-7

marginal income for each sales territory. This marginal income is then apportioned among the products sold in the territory; apportionment among products, like the contribution apportionment among sales territories, is a judgmental decision for which no standard rules can be established. Nevertheless, the territory manager should be in a better position to make this decision than a manager who is in a central office, far removed from territory selling activities. The target marginal income for each product is combined with the standard product cost for the projected sales volume, to

I. Eastern territory
  Target contribution $750,000
  Direct territory fixed costs   100,000

  Desired marginal income $850,000

  Marginal income apportioned to products

	A	B
Marginal income	$400,000	$450,000
Standard product cost	400,000	450,000
Total dollar sales	$800,000	$900,000
Planned unit sales	40,000	30,000
Unit selling price	$20	$30
Current selling price (Figure 10-7)	$18	$31

II. Western territory
  Target contribution $300,000
  Direct territory fixed costs   60,000

  Desired marginal income $360,000

  Marginal income apportioned to products

	A	B
Marginal income	$200,000	$160,000
Standard product cost	200,000	150,000
Total dollar sales	$400,000	$310,000
Planned unit sales	20,000	10,000
Unit selling price	$20	$31
Current selling price (Figure 10-7)	$22	$32

158

III.   Southern Territory
    Target contribution $450,000
    Direct territory fixed costs   75,000

    Desired marginal income $525,000
    Marginal income apportioned to products

	A	B
Marginal income	$225,000	$300,000
Standard product cost	150,000	225,000
Total dollar sales	$375,000	$525,000
Planned unit sales	15,000	15,000
Unit selling price	$25	$35
Current selling price (Figure 10-7)	$20	$30

Figure 10-8

arrive at the total dollar sales for each product. From this sales figure the projected unit selling price is computed.

However, the projected selling price calculated by this procedure provides only a starting point for setting the product selling price. The prices computed for the Eastern Territory, for example, must be evaluated in light of expected competitor actions. If it appears that customers will shift to other suppliers because of the $2 increase in product A prices, the territory manager may have to perform various cost–volume–profit analyses, such as those indicated in Figures 10-5 and 10-6. If these analyses suggest that territory contribution is unlikely to be as high as the target, the central company managers will have to reassess the original apportionment of contribution to sales territories. The central managers may also consider a cost reduction effort to reduce company costs in order to meet the profit target.

A manager can quickly spot unrealistic territory contribution targets with this approach by comparing the computed price with the current selling price. Consider for example, the Southern Territory: the territory manager, to achieve his contribution target, will have to increase the price of each product by $5. If this cannot be done, the company might consider shifting contribution away from the Southern Territory to another territory, such as the Western Territory. This territory will be able to reduce current selling prices and still meet its contribution target; consequently, the Western Territory contribution target can be increased without increasing its product selling prices. Various combinations of changes in cost, volume, or contribution can be evaluated until a satisfactory level of product prices is achieved for each territory.

The role of direct cost and contribution data in this process is one of clearly identifying the impact on contribution and profit of various prices. Direct costs are not used in a rigid formula that automatically computes a selling price.

PRICING FOR SPECIAL OFFERS

The role of direct cost data in special offer decisions is similar to their role in pricing, as just discussed. In special offer decisions, the direct cost data set a price floor below which the company will not want to sell its product, but such data do not determine the upper limit on product prices. Usually, special offers are accepted if the price offered for the product exceeds the direct cost of producing the product. This decision rule is based on the assumption that the company will have greater profits if the price received for the product exceeds the added cost of producing the product. The typical special offer pricing decision is illustrated in Figure 10-9.

In this example a company has a product that generates sufficient demand during eight months of the year to permit the company to sell all 6,000 units it produces each month for its normal unit selling price of $150. During the months of May through August, however, demand is below this level, and the company has excess capacity. During this period the company can improve its profits if it can find additional customers who are willing to pay a price in excess of the direct unit cost of $80. For example, assume that a nonregular customer approaches the company during May with an offer to buy 1,000 units per month for June and July at a unit price of $100. The company may feel that the price is too low for the product; however, if this sale will not detract from regular customer sales, the company will add to its profits by accepting the offer. As the analysis in the third section of Figure 10-9 indicates, the profits of the company will increase by $40,000 if the price offer of $100 is accepted. This profit increase is equal to the difference between the incremental revenue of $200,000 and the increase in cost of $160,000;

This illustration shows how the economic effects of a special offer can be analyzed if there is idle plant capacity; however, the decision maker must take care that special offers do not commit facilities that would have been used for producing products that could be sold at regular prices. For instance, suppose the company that produces product Q is approached at the end of June by a customer who wants to buy 9,000 units of product Q with 3,000 units to be produced and delivered during each of the months of July, August, and September. Before accepting this offer, the decision maker must consider the marginal income given up from regular sales; that is, he must look at the opportunity cost of accepting this special offer. The analysis for this offer is presented in Figure 10-10.

Pricing Special Offers

I. Product Q data

Normal selling price		$150
Direct costs		
Production	$70	
Marketing	10	80
Marginal income per unit		$ 70

II. Product demand information
  A. The plant produces at full capacity, September through April, manufacturing 6,000 units of Product Q each month.
  B. Product demand from regular customers for May through August:

Month	Demand
May	5,000
June	4,000
July	3,000
August	4,500

III. Analysis of special offer
  A. Details of offer: a customer (not a regular customer) offers to purchase 2,000 units at a unit price of $100.
  B. Analysis of offer

Revenue from offer (2,000 units × $100)		$200,000
Direct costs of offer		
Production (2,000 units × $70)	$140,000	
Marketing (2,000 units × $10)	20,000	160,000
Marginal income generated by special offer		$ 40,000

Figure 10-9

I. Details of offer: customer offers to purchase 9,000 units to be produced and delivered at the rate of 3,000 units per month for the months of July, August, and September. The price offered is $100 per unit.

II. Analysis of offer

    A. Revenue from offer (9,000 units × $100) $900,000

    B. Direct costs of offer

Production (9,000 units × $70)	$630,000	
Marketing (9,000 units × $10)	90,000	720,000

    C. Marginal income generated by special offer $180,000

    D. Opportunity cost of accepting offer

July	$ –0–	
August	105,000	
September	210,000	
Total opportunity cost		315,000
Profit effect of accepting special offer		($135,000)

III. Opportunity cost computations

    A. July—no opportunity cost because no regular sales were given up to produce the 3,000 units.

    B. August

Maximum capacity	6,000 units
Normal production	4,500 units
Slack capacity	1,500 units
Capacity required for special offer	3,000 units
Regular sales given up if offer accepted	1,500 units

Opportunity cost (1,500 units × $70 unit marginal income) $105,000

C. September
    Maximum capacity   6,000 units
    Normal production   6,000 units

    Slack capacity   –0–
    Capacity required for special offer 3,000 units

    Regular sales given up if offer accepted 3,000 units

        Opportunity cost (3,000 units $\times$ $70 unit marginal
           income) $210,000

Figure 10-10

First the marginal income generated by the special offer is computed—
$180,000 will be added to company profits if the offer is accepted. Con-
sequently, the individual who is deciding whether to take the offer may be
tempted to accept because the revenue generated by the offer exceeds the
direct costs of the offer. But if he looks further, he will find that the company profits will be lowered by $135,000 when he accepts the offer. This
profit reduction is caused by the large opportunity cost associated with the
normal business given up to accept the special offer. Had the decision
maker in this case focused his attention exclusively on the amount of
marginal income generated by the special offer, he might have accepted the
low-priced offer because revenue generated by the offer exceeded the direct
cost of providing the goods for the customer. The opportunity cost analysis
in this case provides data telling the decision maker that his price on the
special offer is too low. In other words, the decision maker should set a
price for the special offer that provides a positive amount after opportunity
costs are deducted from the marginal income generated by the special offer.

In summary, the cost analysis used in setting prices for special offers
should always include an evaluation of the opportunity cost of accepting
the offer. If the special offer utilizes excess idle capacity, the opportunity
cost is zero; and the price accepted for the special offer should exceed the
direct cost of providing the units requested by the customer. If the special
offer will preempt facilities currently used to produce another product, the
minimum price the company places on its product should exceed both the
direct costs and the opportunity cost incurred if the offer is accepted.

CHAPTER 11

ADDITIONAL APPLICATIONS OF DIRECT COST INFORMATION TO PRICING DECISIONS

Pricing decisions for standard products require analyses that differ from those required for custom product pricing decisions; intracompany pricing decisions require data analyses differing from those used for pricing to outside customers; moreover, a pricing plan is essential if a company is to have a sensible approach to pricing its products. A discussion of these topics shows how direct cost and contribution information can be used to develop useful information for pricing decisions.

PRICING STANDARD AND CUSTOM PRODUCTS

Standard products are mass-produced items, each unit of product having the same characteristics as every other unit. Various types of cameras, boats, bicycles, and so on, fit in this category. In contrast, custom products are made to fit the unique needs of a specific customer. Certain steel castings, special purpose vehicles, and bridges are custom products, since each one is built to the specifications of the customer; and normally the differences in customer needs dictate that each product made be different from the others. The pricing of standard products is explored first, and then the use of direct cost and contribution data for pricing custom products is examined.

One of the primary characteristics of a standard product is its tendency to follow a sales pattern over its life like the curve appearing in Figure 11-1, which depicts the evolutionary life cycle of most standard products. Four stages are identified in this figure: introduction, growth, maturity, and decline. During the introductory period, sales increase slowly, but there is a rapid increase in sales during the growth stage. This volume continues at a high level during the maturity stage, with a drop in sales taking place during the final stage of decline. Pricing strategies vary with the life cycle stage of the product, and the appropriate cost analyses also vary with the life cycle stage.*

The company introducing a product has a wide range of flexibility in setting the price for the new product, and the price the company chooses is significant because the initial price will create a product image that is likely to persist throughout the life of the product. Ideally, the company should choose a price that causes the product to gain wide acceptance quickly and to generate a suitable contribution to company profits. An error that pricing managers should avoid at the introductory stage of a product's life is the use of the wrong cost data for establishing an initial price.

For instance, significant development costs are usually associated with a new product, and the initial unit production costs will be higher than those incurred at the sales volume the company plans to achieve with that product. Figure 11-2 illustrates this point for a product that is to be introduced by the Hypothetical Corporation. The development costs of this new product amount to $36,000, and direct fixed production costs are ex-

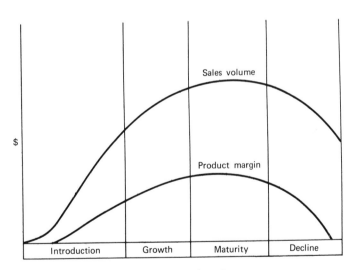

Figure 11-1   Product life cycle: standard products.

* Alfred R. Oxenfeldt, "Establishing Sound Pricing Policies for Profits Planning," *Cost and Management* (June 1964), pp. 263–271. This article includes a clear presentation of the pricing strategies that are appropriate for the various life cycle stages.

Hypothetical Corporation
Pricing Analysis for a New Product

I. Basic data
Development costs direct to product $36,000
Unit product costs

Units Produced Per Month	Unit Cost
below 1,001	$3.00
1,001–3,000	2.50
above 3,000	2.00

Direct fixed production costs per month   1,100
Target monthly contribution during introduction   3,000
   stage

II. Price analysis

Monthly sales volume (units)	1,000	4,000
Desired payback for development costs	12 months	24 months
Target monthly contribution	$ 3,000	$ 3,000
Marginal income to cover development costs	3,000	1,500
Direct fixed costs of production (monthly)	1,100	1,100
Total desired marginal income	$ 7,100	$ 5,600
Total variable production cost	3,000	8,000
Desired sales revenue	$10,100	$13,600
Unit selling price	$10.10	$3.40

Figure 11-2

pected to be $1,100 each month. Unit production costs range from a high of $3, for the initial period of production when volume is low, to a cost of $2, when volume has increased to the point at which the plant is operating efficiently. This reduction in unit cost is not caused by the lower fixed cost per unit at high production volumes; rather, it is attributable to the improvements in production efficiency that occur as a company gains experience in producing a new product, and to the lower level of variable cost associated with production levels that correspond to the designed plant capacity. The managers of Hypothetical Corporation have selected the target monthly contribution of $3,000 as the goal for the introduction stage of new products.

The foregoing data about the new product are combined in the second section of Figure 11-2 to show two different prices that can result from the use of various assumptions about unit cost and development cost payout. The left-hand column gives the introductory product price that should be charged if hypothetical uses unit product costs that are expected during the early stages of production, as well as a short payout period of 12 months for development costs. The combination of these two factors results in an introductory price of $10.10—a price that is almost three times as high as the one ($3.40) in the right-hand column, which is based on expected unit costs at volume production and on a development cost payout period of 24 months.

Since customer resistance to a new product usually varies inversely with product price, the use of the appropriate cost for the initial product price is vital to the success of the product. Obviously, initial unit production costs are inappropriate because they are invariably higher than the unit costs experienced as production approaches the planned plant capacity. Therefore, pricing managers should consider the expected unit cost to be incurred during the growth or maturity stage when they choose an initial introductory product price. Choosing a price on the basis of the initial unit costs and a short payout period for development cost may cause pricing managers to arrive at a price that repels customers, thereby killing the product's chances of developing beyond the introductory stage.

If the product survives the introductory period and moves into the growth stage, the sponsoring company will usually find that a number of competitors are now also producing a very similar item. A market price usually emerges during this stage, with a relatively wide range of market prices early in the stage and a narrow range of market prices near the end of the stage. Sellers of the product during this stage must take competitor prices into account when setting a product price, and the major consideration of the firms producing the product is whether enough sales volume can be generated to justify remaining in the market. Pricing decisions, then, are a matter of selecting the product price that will generate a sales volume sufficient to produce the target contribution amount established by the company.

A large part of the analysis that is relevant for this life cycle stage involves cost–volume–profit analyses similar to those reviewed in Chapter 8. Figure 11-3 illustrates an analysis that relates to the product introduced in Figure 11-2. The product has now reached its growth stage; and the possible product prices range from $5 to $8. The different prices are caused by the product differentiation the various sellers are able to maintain; that

Pricing Analysis for Growth Stage of the Product Life Cycle

I. Basic data
    Standard unit costs
        Above 3,000 units $2.00
        1,000–3,000 units   2.50
    Direct fixed production costs per month $ 1,100
    Planned monthly product contribution   10,000
                                                     ———————
        Total monthly marginal income required $11,100
                                                     ═══════

    Price range
        Low $5.00
        High   8.00
    Estimated monthly sales in units

| | Volume | |
Price	High	Low
$5	4,500	3,500
6	4,000	3,000
7	3,500	2,000
8	3,000	1,500

II. Price Analysis

Price	Marginal Income per Unit	Sales in Units		Total Marginal Income	
		High	Low	High	Low
$5	$3.00	4,500	3,500	$13,500	$10,500
6	4.00	4,000	3,000	16,000	12,000
7	5.00	3,500	2,000	17,500	9,000[a]
8	5.50	3,000	1,500	16,500	8,250

[a] Marginal income per unit of $4.50.

Figure 11-3

is, the seller who can convince buyers that his product is better than that of his competitors can charge a price near the upper end of the price range.

However, the number of units that can be sold at any specific price is uncertain, and the pricing managers should evaluate the product contribution that will be generated under the high and low estimates of sales volume for the various unit prices. For example, marginal income can vary from a low of $10,500 to a high of $13,500 with a unit price of $5, and it can vary from $8,250 to $16,500 with a unit price of $8. When these amounts are compared with the target monthly marginal income of $11,100, the pricing manager can see which price is likely to permit him to reach his target. In this example, a price of $6 has a low marginal income of $12,000, which is above the required monthly marginal income of $11,100. Consequently, if the pricing manager selects the $6 price, he is certain to meet his contribution target. The high marginal income for this price is $16,000; but if the pricing manager is willing to take some risk, he can set his price at $7, since the high marginal income that can be earned from this price is $17,500 (although it could go as low as $9,000). Probability estimates could be used in this case to weight the various sales volumes that could occur between the high and low, but the basic idea of using a sales volume range instead of a single estimate is the same regardless of whether probability estimates are used.*

As the product matures, the range of prices at which the product can be sold narrows, and customers become aware of and sensitive to price differences. Many customers begin to consider the different brands of the product to be essentially equal in quality, and they begin to buy the product almost entirely on the basis of price. Because of this sensitivity to price, customers shift their purchases to the company that provides the product at the lowest price. Accordingly, the companies producing the product begin to look for ways to reduce production cost as a means of maintaining planned product contribution levels.

Consider the product that was introduced in Figure 11-2 with a standard unit cost of $2 for production levels above 3,000 units per month. As this product matures and price competition becomes strong, the company may decide to substitute a lower quality material for the one currently used. This reduces the quality of the product slightly; but since customers tend to equate quality across all brands, the quality reduction has little impact on sales.

To determine the product contribution impact from the use of cheaper materials and the elimination of several labor operations, the pricing manager can prepare an analysis like that in the second section of Figure 11-4. Here the monthly marginal incomes are computed for the various price levels for the current standard unit cost of $2.00 and for the $1.70 unit cost that will be incurred if the product is modified. At the $2.00 unit cost, none of the marginal income amounts are as high as the $12,100 planned marginal income; however, the reduction in unit cost causes an increase

---

* Robert Schlaifer, *Probability and Statistics for Business Decisions* (New York: McGraw-Hill, 1959). This book contains a comprehensive discussion of the use of probability estimates in decision making.

I. Basic data
   Standard unit cost (units currently being produced)

Material	$1.20
Labor	.60
Overhead	.20
	$2.00

   Standard unit cost for modified product

Material	$1.00
Labor	.50
Overhead	.20
	$1.70

   Estimated monthly sales volume

Price	Volume
$4.00	6,000
4.25	5,000
4.50	4,500
4.75	4,000

Planned monthly product contribution	$11,000
Direct fixed production cost per month	1,100
Total monthly marginal income required	$12,100

II. Price analysis
   Planned monthly marginal income without product modification

Price	Units Sold	Marginal Income per unit	Total Marginal Income
$4.00	6,000	$2.00	$12,000
4.25	5,000	2.25	11,250
4.50	4,500	2.50	11,250
4.75	4,000	2.75	11,000

Planned monthly marginal income with product modification

Price	Units Sold	Marginal Income per unit	Total Marginal Income
$4.00	6,000	$2.30	$13,800
4.25	5,000	2.55	12,750
4.50	4,500	2.80	12,600
4.75	4,000	3.05	12,200

Figure 11-4

in projected marginal income sufficient to give the pricing manager flexibility in setting his price while still meeting his required monthly marginal income target. That is, the estimated marginal income generated each month exceeds the target of $12,100 regardless of the price selected. If there is a great deal of uncertainty about how many units can be sold at each price, high and low sales estimates can be incorporated in the analysis to highlight the best and the worst that are expected to occur with each price.

During the final, declining phase of the product life, direct costs are critical to the pricing decision because they help determine when the company will stop producing the product. During this phase of the product's life the pricing decisions become mainly output and investment decisions. That is, the decision involves the selection of a price below which the company will no longer produce the product.

One way of developing this price involves the use of contribution targets. Figure 11-5 contains an analysis that illustrates this approach. In this example the desired monthly marginal income ($3,100) is computed from the direct fixed costs ($1,100) and the contribution target ($2,000). Note that the target contribution for the declining product is much lower than $11,000, which was used for the mature product. The price analysis in the second half of Figure 11-5 indicates that any price above $2.40 will enable the company to meet its contribution target and that a price of $2.60 will generate the maximum marginal income.

However, because products in the declining stage generate a low contribution, the pricing managers must constantly decide whether the contribution generated by the product is sufficient to justify its continued production, even if the product is generating more than the target amount of contribution. In other words, the pricing decision for declining products

Price Analysis for Declining Products

I. Basic data

    Standard unit cost, $1.70

Direct fixed production costs per month	$1,100
Planned monthly product contribution	2,000
Total monthly marginal income required	$3,100

    Estimated monthly sales

Price	Volume
$2.20	5,000
2.40	4,500
2.60	4,000
2.80	3,000

II. Price analysis

Price	Units Sold	Marginal Income per Unit	Total Marginal Income
$2.20	5,000	$ .50	$2,500
2.40	4,500	.70	3,150
2.60	4,000	.90	3,600
2.80	3,000	1.10	3,300

Figure 11-5

involves an assessment of the most profitable use of the facilities used to produce the declining product. For instance, consider the case of the product illustrated in Figure 11–5. This product has the capability of providing a monthly contribution in excess of the established target. But the pricing manager should examine the opportunity cost of producing the declining product, in addition to making sure the product contribution is equal to the contribution target.

Suppose, for example, that the facilities used to produce the declining product could be used to make the product dealt with in Figure 11–6. This product has been introduced and is now entering its growth stage; however, the company does not have slack capacity with which to produce the product. Accordingly, if the company continues to produce the declining product, the price charged should enable this product to generate a contribution equal to or greater than the new product.

I. Basic data

   The facilities currently being used to produce the product described in Figure 11-5 can be used to produce the product analyzed below, which is entering its growth stage.

   Standard unit cost $4

   Direct fixed production costs per month $13,000

   Estimated monthly sales

	Volume	
Price	High	Low
$10	6,500	3,500
11	6,000	3,000
12	5,500	2,500
13	5,000	2,000

II. Price analysis for new product

Price	Marginal Income per Unit	Sales (units)		Total Marginal Income	
		High	Low	High	Low
$10	6	6,500	3,500	39,000	21,000
11	7	6,000	3,000	42,000	21,000
12	8	5,500	2,500	44,000	20,000
13	9	5,000	2,000	45,000	18,000

III. Evaluation of continued production of old product

   Maximum expected product contribution from old product (Figure 11-5)

Marginal income for price of $2.60	$ 3,600	
Direct fixed production costs	1,100	
Product contribution		$2,500

   Minimum product contribution from new product

Marginal income for a price of $13	$18,000	
Direct fixed production cost	13,000	
Product contribution		5,000

Minimum opportunity loss of continuing to produce declining product	$2,500

Figure 11-6

173

The first section of Figure 11-6 shows the unit costs and fixed costs direct to the new product, as well as the sales volume estimates. A price analysis for the new product is contained in the second section of the figure, followed by an opportunity cost evaluation of continuing the declining product. Since the best possible marginal income ($3,600) of the declining product and the worst marginal income ($18,000) of the new product are used in this evaluation, the estimate of the opportunity cost is as conservative as possible. Monthly product contribution for the declining product is $2,500, and for the new product is $5,000. Therefore, the opportunity cost of continuing the declining product is $5,000; and if this amount is deducted from the $2,500 product contribution made by the declining product, we have an opportunity loss of $2,500. In this example, then, the company should stop producing the declining product unless the price of that product can be increased enough to cover the $2,500 opportunity loss. Otherwise, the declining product should be dropped, even though it is providing a contribution in excess of the target amount.

The product life cycle is very important to pricing decisions for standard products, and the accountant who prepares studies for pricing managers should tailor his analyses to fit the life cycle stage of each product for which he develops an analysis. The accountant may argue that he cannot reliably pinpoint the specific life cycle stage for a product; however, he should remember that it is better to make a crude estimate of the life cycle stage of a product than to ignore the complexities of the product life cycle in the hope that they will disappear.

Product life cycles are not too important in pricing custom products because each product is unique, and because of this uniqueness there is no well-established market price to which the pricing manager can refer for guidance in setting his price. However, if he charges a price that is too high, his customers will go elsewhere; and if he charges a price that is too low, his order backlog will grow tremendously. Consequently, the pricing manager for custom products can use the price he charges to ration his productive facilities among his customers. Direct cost and contribution data serve these decisions by showing the marginal income and contribution provided by each job and by each unit of the constraining factor.

Consider the case of the company in Figure 11-7 with three machines that produce custom products for the customers. Each machine has a capacity that can be used to make products to customer order. Assume that this company wants to maintain an equal backlog of work for each machine and that it is not interested in accumulating for any machine an order backlog greater than 12 months. In this case the company can use a sliding scale of marginal income per hour amounts to compute prices that balance the order backlog for the three machines.

The scale for each machine starts with a zero marginal income per hour if there is no order backlog, and it rises until it reaches a high enough level to drive away customers as the backlog reaches 12 months. Thus machine 1 in Figure 11–7 has a marginal income per machine hour of zero for order backlogs of less than 2 months and a marginal income per machine hour of $80 for a backlog that exceeds 12 months. Note that the marginal income amounts per machine hour vary from one machine to another. These variations occur because of the desire to balance the accumulated work backlog for all three machines. If the marginal income per hour were the same for all machines, customers would place orders in such a manner that the backlog for machine 3 would always be greater than for machine 1. These hourly rates are based on an analysis of past history and on the judgment of the company's pricing managers.

Because of the increasing marginal income per machine hour as the backlog increases, the price charged for a particular job will vary with the order backlog size of the machines that will be used to produce the product. As the backlog drops, a lower price is charged for the work done on that machine. In other words, the company charges a low price when there is excess capacity, and it charges a high price when there is little slack capacity.

Marginal Income per Machine Hour for Custom
Product Pricing

Backlog (Months)	Marginal Income per Machine Hour		
	Machine 1	Machine 2	Machine 3
0–2	$ 0	$ 0	$ 0
2–4	10	10	20
4–6	20	30	40
6–8	30	50	60
8–10	40	70	80
10–12	50	90	100
over 12	80	150	180

Figure 11-7

I.   Basic data for job 124 and job 235
     Direct job costs
          Material $24,000
          Labor   16,000
          Overhead   7,000
                          _____
          Total $47,000
                          ========

     Machined hours required for job
          Machine 1,   100
          Machine 2,   200
          Machine 3,   50
II. Order backlog
     Job 124
          Machine 1,   7 months
          Machine 2,   3 months
          Machine 3,   9 months
     Job 235
          Machine 1,   11 months
          Machine 2,   9 months
          Machine 3,   over 12 months
III. Price calculations
     Price computation for job 124
          Direct product costs $47,000
          Desired marginal income
               Machine 1   (100 × $30) $ 3,000
               Machine 2   (200 × $10)   2,000
               Machine 3   (50 × $80)   4,000   9,000
                                             _____   _____
               Price for job 124 $56,000
                                                           ========

     Price computation for job 235
          Direct product costs $47,000
          Desired marginal income
               Machine 1   (100 × $50) $ 5,000
               Machine 2   (200 × $70)   14,000
               Machine 3   (50 × $180)   9,000   28,000
                                             _____   _____
          Price for job 235 $75,000
                                                           ========

Figure 11-8

Figure 11-8 shows how this method can be used to compute the prices for two different jobs. Job 124 is priced for a period during which the company has a relatively low backlog of orders, and job 235 is priced for a period during which there is little slack capacity. The prices for jobs 124 and 235 are developed through a combination of direct job costs and desired marginal incomes for each machine that works on the job. The direct costs of $47,000 consist of the estimated amounts of material, labor, and overhead costs that are directly traceable to the job. The pricing manager computes the desired marginal income by referring to the accumulated order backlog for each machine. He next refers to Figure 11-7 for the desired hourly marginal income rate, and this rate is multiplied by the number of hours that will be required for the job to arrive at the total desired marginal income for the job. The amount obtained is added to the direct costs to compute the price to charge for the job.

Note that the direct costs and the machine time required for the two jobs are the same, but the prices that are computed for the two jobs are significantly different. Job 124 has a price of $56,000, whereas job 235 has a price of $75,000. This difference is caused because more slack capacity was available when the price was developed for 124 than was available when the price was developed for job 235. In other words, the price charged for the product goes up as the supply of machine time decreases; consequently, the customers who are unwilling to pay the high prices for the scarce machine hours will go elsewhere for their products, or they will wait until there is slack capacity and lower prices. In this case the desired marginal income is used to compute a price that rations the machine hours among customers in the manner desired by the company management. Obviously, the desired marginal income per machine hour scales would have to be continuously reviewed to ensure that the prices were achieving the objectives of balanced machine backlog and an absolute backlog of no more than 12 months.

Another approach for pricing custom products refers to the marginal income that is currently being earned for each unit of constraining factor. Consider the case of the company illustrated in Figure 11-9; this company has three machines that are used in manufacturing products to customer specifications, and most jobs use some time on each machine. The jobs already accepted for the current time period and the time each job requires on each machine appear in the first section of the figure.

Assume that jobs E and F in Figure 11-9 are received and that prices must be quoted on these jobs. Since job E uses the slack hours remaining for machine 2, this job should earn an hourly marginal income that is at least as high as the highest hourly marginal income currently earned on that machine. Since job C is currently generating the highest marginal in-

I. Basic data

Machine capacity (hours per month)

	Total Capacity	Committed	Slack
Machine 1	1,200	800	400
Machine 2	2,000	1,900	100
Machine 3	900	400	500

Jobs accepted

	Total Marginal Income	Time Required for Jobs Accepted		
		Machine 1	Machine 2	Machine 3
Job A	$ 5,000	100	500	50
Job B	6,000	150	300	150
Job C	21,000	350	700	70
Job D	5,200	200	400	130
Total		800	1,900	400

Marginal income per machine hour

	Machine 1	Machine 2	Machine 3
Job A	$50	$10	$100
Job B	40	20	40
Job C	60	30	300
Job D	26	13	40

II. Price computations

Job E

Direct costs	$40,000

Machine time required
Machine 1, 200
Machine 2, 100
Machine 3, 300

Job E price

Direct costs	$40,000
Marginal income (100 × 30)	3,000
Minimum price	$43,000

Job F
 Direct costs $30,000
 Machine time required
  Machine 1,   200
  Machine 2,   0
  Machine 3,   100
Job F price
 Direct costs $30,000
 Marginal income (200 × 60)   12,000

    Minimum price   42,000

Figure 11-9

come per machine hour ($30), the 100 hours of machine 2 slack time are multiplied by $30 to compute the minimum marginal income for the job. Job F uses none of the time on machine 2, but it uses all the slack time remaining on machine 1 (after the time required for job E is considered). Accordingly, machine 1 becomes the constraining factor for this job, and the highest marginal income currently earned per hour on this machine is $60. When this amount is applied to the 200 hours of time required on this machine, a desired marginal income of $12,000 results; and a price of $42,000 is computed for the job.

Instead of relying for his price computations solely on the marginal income per unit of the constraining factor, the pricing manager could refer to the marginal income per machine hour that each job provides. He might, for example, take the highest marginal income per hour being generated by each machine and use the rate that results in the greatest amount of marginal income for the job. This might be especially useful if the customer normally haggles over the price. The pricing manager could base his opening price on the highest marginal income that he computed, and he could compute his minimum acceptable price for the job on the basis of the maximum marginal income earned per unit of the constraining factor. In any event, pricing computations that are based on marginal income per unit of capacity provide a pricing guide that helps the pricing manager to make sound decisions on pricing custom products.

INTRACOMPANY PRICING

Custom product pricing decisions are not easy, but they probably create less discord and infighting than decisions on pricing policies for products that are shifted from one part of the company to another.* Rather than approaching this topic from the viewpoint that there is a correct transfer price policy, we argue here that the transfer price policy of a company depends on the segment performance evaluation scheme followed by a company. For instance, if all company segments are evaluated on their profit performance, the transfer price that the selling division charges the buying division must include some amount of profit. This creates problems if the division selling to the customer must make special prices from time to time. If a division sells at the price it paid to the producing division, it may lose the sale; if the division sells below the price it paid to the producing division and if that price is above the direct unit cost of the product, the company still earns a positive contribution from the sale.

This problem can be avoided if the company evaluates the performance of revenue generating segments on their ability to meet contribution targets, and if it evaluates producing departments on the basis of their ability to produce the goods at standard costs. In this type of evaluation scheme, the standard direct unit cost is the amount that is transferred from the producing segment to the revenue generating segment. This approach follows the concept of responsibility accounting discussed in Chapter 4. That is, the costs are charged to the segments in which the decisions that cause them to be incurred are made, and the revenues generated are credited to the segments in which the decisions were made that caused the revenues to be produced. A revenue generating segment is charged with the standard direct cost of a unit of product because the sales personnel in that segment cause the company to incur that amount of cost each time a sale is made. No standard cost variances are transferred to the revenue generating segments because the decisions that cause these variances to occur are made in the production segments of the firm.

However, a company that wishes to evaluate the performance of all segments on profitability can use direct cost information to help make its transfer price system a workable one. This can be done by using what might be called a dual transfer price: two prices would move with each unit transferred from a producing to a selling segment—one price is the standard direct unit cost, and the other is the price used for computing segment profitability. This transfer pricing approach provides information to the selling segment that allows it to make sound pricing decisions when quoting reduced prices to customers, and it allows a profit to be computed for the producing segment.

* Hector R. Anton and Peter A. Firmin, *Contemporary Issues in Cost Accounting* (Boston:, Houghton Mifflin 1972). This book presents several readings on the subject of intracompany pricing, and it includes a comprehensive bibliography on the subject.

Figure 11–10 demonstrates how this transfer pricing policy works. In this illustration the revenue generating segment receives an offer from a customer to purchase 2,000 units at a price of $70, which is below the $75 transfer price used for performance evaluation. If the revenue generating segment received only the $75 transfer price, it would reject the offer because of the apparent $10,000 loss. However, if the selling segment also receives the standard direct unit cost information, it will accept the offer because of the $40,000 marginal income generated by the sale for the company as a whole.

Some companies use absorption cost data for transfer prices on the assumption that these data encourage salesmen to maintain high prices for the product. But just the opposite may happen. Wilmer Wright states that some companies have found that sales personnel assume that all overhead expenses in the unit cost are fixed; as a result, the salesmen accept prices that cover only the labor and material cost.* Using the dual transfer price avoids this problem because the salesmen can see how much a unit of

Dual Transfer Prices

I. Basic data
Standard direct unit cost	$ 50
Transfer price used for performance evaluation	$ 75
Normal selling price to customer	$100

II. Evaluation of special offer by revenue generating segment
   Customer offers to pay $70 per unit for 2,000 units
   Evaluation using performance evaluation price

Revenue (2,000 × $70)	$140,000
Revenue segment cost (2,000 × $75)	150,000
Revenue segment loss	($10,000)

   Evaluation using standard direct unit cost

Revenue (2,000 × $70)	$140,000
Cost (2,000 × $50)	100,000
Marginal income	$ 40,000

Figure 11-10

* Wilmer Wright, "Direct Costs Are Better for Pricing,"*NAA Bulletin* (*Formerly Management Accounting*) (April 1960), pp. 17–26.

product costs the company and can make their pricing decisions accordingly.

THE PRICING PLAN

Prices are clearly related to profits, and profit planning and price planning are closely interrelated. Price planning does not mean that a company decides in advance how much to charge for an item and then sticks to that price; instead, price planning requires a great deal of flexibility, to permit adjustment of individual product prices to meet changing conditions.

The following ingredients of a pricing plan have been developed by Alfred Oxenfeldt.†

1. *Price objectives.* The basic objectives of the company are reflected in its pricing objectives. For example, does the company want to use its prices to earn a certain rate of return? Does the company want to obtain broad market coverage, or does it want to cover a select part of the market?

2. *Evaluation of market situation.* This part of the plan should include a review of the recent price behavior of competitors. The attitudes of customers toward the company prices should be compared with their attitude toward competitor's prices. The company should identify the customers who are concerned about prices, and their likely behavior, as well as the customers who are likely to be unconcerned about a price increase.

3. *Review and appraisal of current pricing practices.* The company should review its current pricing practices in light of the information it has developed in step 2 of the pricing plan.

4. *Forecast of market and price conditions.* The probable price actions of individual competitors should be forecast, and the products and markets in which there is likely to be price changes should be identified.

5. *Preparation of alternative pricing programs.* Individual products and marketing areas should be selected, and cost–volume–profit analyses should be developed for several different price levels.

6. *Selection of specific pricing strategy.* A pricing strategy should be selected for each product and market, and the assumptions underlying that strategy should be explicitly stated, thus allowing prices to be adjusted as soon as an assumption proves to be invalid.

7. *Implementation of the price program.* Time schedules, responsibility assignments, and so on, should be prepared to assure that the pricing plan is properly implemented.

† Alfred R. Oxenfeldt, *ibid.*, pp. 264–265.

8. *Establishment of a review and control program.* Effectiveness measures should be identified, and the circumstances under which the plan can be changed should be clearly set forth.

In summary, the pricing plan consists of a series of steps leading to careful decisions at a number of critical points in the pricing process. It provides a flexible guide to profitable pricing decisions, and it helps reduce the number of unexpected price changes encountered by the firm.

CHAPTER 12

DIRECT COSTING FOR SERVICE INDUSTRIES

Almost all the literature on direct costing is devoted to the use of the direct costing technique in manufacturing firms. Yet the concepts of direct cost and contribution analysis are equally applicable to firms that produce no physical products (i.e., service companies). In this chapter, a discussion of the characteristics of service companies is followed by an illustration of how direct cost data are useful in hospitals and in banks.

SERVICE INDUSTRY CHARACTERISTICS

One of the most prominent characteristics of service companies is their lack of product that can be inventoried. They provide services that cannot be accumulated in inventory but must be produced coincident with their sale. Cashing a check for a customer is a service a bank provides, and this service is produced simultaneously with the sale of the service. The same is true for the hospital that provides nursing care to a patient; the care is produced at the same time it is sold. Because it cannot accumulate a stockpile of the services it sells, the service business is concerned with having just the amount of productive capacity that is needed to meet the demand for its service.

A manufacturing firm can change its output or inventory to match fluctuations in demand, but its productive capacity will remain relatively constant for extended periods of time. A service firm, on the other hand, varies its output by changing its capacity to produce. Short-term planning decisions for manufacturing firms involve the utilization of productive capacity, and short-term planning decisions for service firms are concerned with planning the desired amount of productive capacity needed to meet demand.

Since variable costs are normally incurred to use productive capacity, planning and controlling variable costs is important to a manufacturing firm. A service firm, in contrast, has so few variable costs direct to the product it sells that such costs can almost be ignored in the majority of planning and control decisions. The direct costs of processing a check by a bank are so small they are negligible; the same is true for the direct costs of processing a loan application or the costs of processing the admittance of a patient to a hospital. Direct costs of cleaning a hotel room are quite small in relation to the daily rates charged for the room. The significant costs for planning and control in service businesses are the planned fixed and semifixed expenses. These are the costs that are associated with productive capacity.

A nursing station in a hospital can vary the number of nurses who work at that station, but a whole nurse must be added when additional nursing care is needed. Thus the cost of nursing care can fluctuate with the number of patients at the nursing station, but not in direct proportion to the number of patients. As each nurse is added to the nursing station, that station increases its capacity to serve an additional number of patients; and until that added capacity is used up, no more nurses are needed at the station, even though additional patients are assigned to the station. The same holds true for reductions in the number of patients at a nursing station. As the number of patients declines, the nursing staff can be reduced by one nurse whenever enough patients are discharged to make excess capacity equal to one nurse.

In banks, the number of tellers can be varied, but not on an hour-by-hour basis or even on a day-to-day basis. Increases in the volume of transactions handled by tellers can be taken care of by a given staff until the service capacity of the existing staff is reached; then capacity is increased by one more teller. The additional person adds one more layer to the existing fixed costs and provides an additional increment of capacity that accommodates additional increases in the volume of services provided.

Personnel cost for an organization segment can be converted to a semifixed behavior pattern from a fixed pattern through the use of central labor pools or through the cross-training of employees to enable them to work in different organization segments. If a central labor pool is used, the various organization segments that draw on this pool to augment productive capacity for peak activity levels increase their fixed cost during the period of peak activity. After this volume declines to a lower level, the employee is returned to the central pool. Although the cost of employees in the central pool is a fixed cost from the viewpoint of the organization as a whole, this procedure should result in a level of company fixed costs lower than it would be if each organization segment maintained a fixed staff with its attendant level of fixed cost. Allowing organization segments to draw employees from a central pool increases the frequency of decisions that affect personnel cost. This increased frequency of decisions increases the number of opportunities that the segment managers have to reduce the expense. As a result, each segment manager, by reducing his personnel cost to the lowest possible level, causes total company personnel cost to reach the lowest possible level.

Although the cost behavior patterns for service businesses differ from those of manufacturing firms, responsibility accounting in a service business is similar to that in a manufacturing firm. The accounting system in a service business should identify cost and revenue changes with the decisions that cause them to change. Joint cost responsibility problems in service industries are solved in the same manner as in manufacturing industries, and the identification of direct and indirect responsibility for costs and revenues is just as important in a service business as in a manufacturing firm. With this discussion of the general characteristics of service businesses as a background, let us review the uses of direct cost concepts in a hospital.

APPLICATION OF DIRECT COST CONCEPTS TO HOSPITAL ACTIVITIES

Hospitals provide a wide array of services to their patients, ranging from sophisticated diagnostic procedures to such simple matters as serving meals. This discussion begins with an illustration of the application of direct cost concepts to a nursing station in a hospital, since this example demonstrates how direct cost concepts work in one of the most critical problem areas of the hospital—control of manpower costs. Later, the use of hospital direct cost information for special offers is illustrated.

One of the first requirements for the use of direct cost concepts in a hospital nursing station is a staffing plan (see Figure 12-1), which indicates the personnel cost and time standards for various volumes of activity, activity in this case being measured in patient days. The first section of Figure 12-1 shows the standard daily cost of the various nursing skills. The costs include wages plus fringe benefits; that is, the costs show how much total hospital costs will increase if a nurse works one day. The second section of the figure includes the time standards that are developed from historical experience, from engineering studies, or from nursing management's best estimate. These time standards are based on the assumption that nursing staff levels can be varied as the patient load at the nursing station varies. The personnel cost is fixed at one of three levels, however; it does not increase or decrease smoothly as the patient level changes, because the nursing personnel cost is a semifixed expense that increases or decreases in a lump sum as selected levels of activity are reached. These time standards could be further refined to show personnel standards by shift.

The time standards and the cost standards are combined in the third section of Figure 12-1 to arrive at the standard daily personnel cost for the three activity ranges. These amounts show the level of fixed costs that the hospital plans to incur for each of three activity levels at the nursing

Nursing Station: Third East Personnel Standards

I. Daily personnel costs

Head nurse	$40
Registered nurse	30
Licensed practical nurse	25
Aides	20

II. Daily personnel requirements, 24-hour period

	Patient Days		
	Below 30	30–35	36–40
Head nurse	1	1	1
Registered nurse	6	6	7
Licensed practical nurse	6	7	8
Aides	4	8	10

III. Budgeted daily personnel costs

	Patient Days		
	Below 30	30–35	36–40
Head nurse	$ 40	$ 40	$ 40
Registered nurse	180	180	210
Licensed practical nurse	150	175	200
Aides	80	160	200
Total	$450	$555	$650

Figure 12-1

Nursing Station: Third East
Rate and Amount Budget

Supervisor: M. Nurse   Period: Month
                                        Base: Patient days

Account	Rate	Amount
Meals		
Breakfast	$ .40	$ -0-
Lunch	.45	-0-
Dinner	.50	-0-
Supplies	.20	30.00
Drugs	.15	20.00
Laundry	.65	40.00
	$2.35	$90.00

Figure 12-2

station: for fewer than 30 patients it expects to spend $450 per day; it plans to spend $555 per day for nursing care for a patient level of 30 to 35; and it expects to spend $650 per day for nursing care if more than 35 patients are assigned to the nursing station.

To complete the budget for this nursing station, the rate and amount budget illustrated in Figure 12-2 must be prepared. This budget shows the increase in total hospital costs ($2.35) from adding one more patient day to Third East, and it gives the fixed amount incurred each month, regardless of the number of patients at the station. The meal costs are computed from the cost standards established for the meals served in the hospital. These standards are used to separate the joint responsibility for meal costs; that is, cost variances of meal production are charged to food services and excessive use of meals is charged to the respective nursing stations. The supplies and drug expenses are developed from one of the cost measurements techniques (scattergraph, least squares, or semiaverage) discussed in Chapter 3. The laundry expense is developed from an analysis of the quantity of laundry needed for each patient day. The direct cost of processing the laundry is applied to this quantity to compute the direct laundry cost of providing one patient day of care. The monthly amount is developed the same way.

The personnel standards and the rate and amount budget can be used to project total costs for the nursing station for various patient day levels. For example, Figure 12-3 shows how costs can be projected for Third East for an estimated patient level of 900 patient days for the coming month. The projected nursing cost is computed by estimating the number of days that nursing cost is expected to fall into each of the three levels. The nursing cost is a semifixed cost, and therefore it must be computed in this manner; if it were a variable cost, the variable cost per patient day would simply be

Nursing Station: Third East
Projected Costs

I. Patient day forecast

Patient Day Level	Days
Below 30	5
30–35	10
36–40	15
Total	30
Total projected patient days	900

II. Expense forecast

Account	Amount
Head nurse	$ 1,200
Registered nurse	5,850
Licensed practical nurse	5,500
Aides	5,000
Meals	
Breakfast	360
Lunch	405
Dinner	450
Supplies	210
Drugs	155
Laundry	625
Total	$19,755

Figure 12-3

Nursing Station: Third East
Performance Report

Supervisor: M. Nurse

Period: Month
Base: Patient days

I. Patient days for the month

Patient Day Level	Days
Below 30	4
30–35	10
35–40	16
Total	30
Total actual patient days	940

II. Actual costs charged to Third East

Account	Amount
Head nurse	$ 1,320
Registered nurse	5,680
Licensed practical nurse	5,425
Aides	5,040
Meals	
Breakfast	401
Lunch	463
Dinner	500
Supplies	258
Drugs	141
Laundry	666
Total	$19,894

III. Performance report

Account	Budget	Variance
Head nurse	$ 1,200	$(120)
Registered nurse	5,880	200
Licensed practical nurse	5,550	125
Aides	5,120	80
Meals		
Breakfast	376	(25)
Lunch	423	(40)
Dinner	470	(30)
Supplies	218	(40)
Drugs	161	20
Laundry	651	(15)
Total	$20,049	$ 155

Figure 12-4

multiplied by the number of patient days. However, a semifixed cost computation requires a count of the number of time periods that the expense is expected to remain at each of the three levels. The summation of time periods by cost levels provides the total expected cost.

Total meal cost, because it is a variable cost, is computed by multiplying the meal cost per patient day by the estimated patient days. The semivariable expense amounts are computed in a similar fashion—the variable rates are multiplied by the patient days, and the fixed amounts are added to this product. The result of these computations is an expense forecast for the nursing station of $19,755. Similar expense forecasts are made for all hospital segments, to arrive at the total estimated cost for the planning period.

The same standards and budgets used to prepare the expense forecast also serve in developing a performance report for the nursing station (see Figure 12-4). The budget amounts in this report are computed in the same manner that was used to develop the forecast expense amounts in Figure 12-3. This report allows the head nurse for Third East to pinpoint the dollar amount of each variance and the type of factor causing the variance. She can see that registered nurse expense is $200 below the budget and that licensed practical nurse expense is $125 below the budgeted amount. An

I. Details of offer from health maintenance organization

The health maintenance organization offers $50 per day for nursing care; the organization expects to send 10 patients per day to the hospital for 20 days during the month and 15 patients per day for the remaining 10 days of the month.

II. Relevant hospital data

The hospital will care for the patients at nursing station Third East, where the normal rate is $75 per patient day.

Twenty-four patients per day are expected at the nursing station during the month if no health maintenance organization patients are accepted.

Cost data

Nursing costs (Figure 12-1)

Patient Day Level	Amount
Below 30	$450
30–35	555
35–40	650

Rate and amount budget (Figure 12-2)

Rate per patient day	$ 2.35
Amount per month	90.00

III. Analysis of health maintenance organization offer

Added costs of caring for patients

Nursing cost increase

Cost with new patients

20 days × $555	$11,100	
10 days × $650	6,500	$17,600.00

Cost without new patients

30 × 450	13,500.00

Total nursing cost increase	$ 4,100.00

Nonnursing cost increase

Total added patient days

20 × 10	200
10 × 15	150
	350

Cost increase	
350 × $2.35	822.50
Total increase in hospital cost	$ 4,922.50
Total added revenue from patients (350 × $50)	$17,500.00
Total added costs from patients	4,922.50
Contribution	$12,577.50

Figure 12-5

investigation of these variances will indicate whether the nursing staff is being used efficiently. The variances for meals are all unfavorable, but these variances average about one dollar per day, which is a relatively insignificant amount. The variances for the other items are also relatively small, and the head nurse will probably direct most of her effort to watching nursing personnel costs.

In addition to the planning and controlling functions that these budget standards serve, they can also be used for pricing hospital services—when, for example, a health maintenance organization approaches a hospital to purchase hospital services. Health maintenance organizations are independent business units that provide medical care to their subscribers. Such organizations usually operate clinics and employ doctors to staff them. Whenever a patient requires hospitalization, the health maintenance organization purchases the necessary hospital care from a local hospital. However, instead of paying the normal rates charged by the hospital, the health maintenance organization will usually try to bargain with the hospital for a lower rate. In these cases, the hospital must know how much its costs will increase for the services the health maintenance organization wants to purchase.

Consider the offer received by one hospital and illustrated in the first section of Figure 12-5. The hospital has been offered $50 per patient day to care for a group of patients; this rate is $25 below the rate of $75 per patient day that is normally charged for patient care. At first glance the hospital management may be inclined to reject the offer on the grounds that is is too low. However, the hospital will have better profits from accepting the offer if the beds at Third East would remain vacant without the added patients. If the beds would remain empty, the hospital can earn

$12,577.50 of contribution by accepting the offer, even though the rate offered is far below its normal rate.

The $12,577.50 added contribution is computed by comparing the cost increase required to care for the patients to the revenue received for rendering the care. Without the additional patients, the hospital would pay $450 per day for nursing costs because there will be fewer than 30 patients at Third East each day. However, accepting the health maintenance organization patients would increase daily nursing cost to $555 per day for the 20 days that 10 patients remain in the hospital, and costs would increase to $650 per day for the 10 days that 15 patients spend in the hospital. Consequently, nursing cost at Third East would be $13,500 without the added patients, and it would be $17,600 with the added patients, an increase of $4,100 in nursing cost. To this amount, the $822.50 variable cost of providing for the additional 350 patient days of service is added, for a total cost increase of $4,922.50. Since revenue increases by $17,500 for the same increase in services, the hospital is $12,577.50 more profitable if it accepts the offer.

This type of analysis can be quickly performed for the hospital with a direct cost system, because costs are already identified by behavior patterns and no special analyses are required to separate costs into fixed and variable components. Moreover, since cost interrelationships between departments are clearly defined, the change in total hospital costs from a change in patient load at any nursing station can be identified rapidly by referring to the budget for that nursing station only. Laundry costs, food service costs, and drug costs that change with the patient level are in the budgets of the individual nursing stations. Thus just as the change in total factory costs from a change in activity in one department can be computed by referring to the budget for that department, the change in total hospital costs from a change in activity in one segment can be computed from the budget for that segment.

APPLICATION OF DIRECT COST CONCEPTS TO BANKING ACTIVITIES

The hospital industry provides one example of the application of direct cost data to a service business, and the banking industry furnishes another illustration of the usefulness of such data for decision making. Of the many services provided by banks, the lending function is probably the most important to the bank's profitability. Because lending is so significant for a bank, this section focuses on a method of utilizing contribution analysis and reporting for planning and controlling lending activities.

The lending activities of a bank are analogous to the marketing activities of a production firm. In a production firm the goods produced by the production function are sold through the marketing function; in a bank the dollars loaned by the lending officers are "produced" by the fund acquisition function of the bank. Since fund acquisition is usually the responsibility of a group of managers who do not make loans, the price at which funds are transferred from the acquisition function to the lending function is the fund transfer price. Moreover, the fund acquisition function and the lending function are jointly responsible for the total expenditures on fund acquisition, and standard cost techniques can be used to separate this joint responsibility in the same way that the material cost responsibility in a manufacturing firm is divided between the purchasing and manufacturing activities.

The primary variable cost of the lending function of a bank is the cost of the funds loaned. That is, the higher the volume of loans, the greater the total cost of the funds that are used to make the loans. Certain additional costs, such as bad debts, will also vary directly with the dollar volume of

Loan Department Contribution

Interest on loans	$700,000
Cost of funds loaned	400,000
Bad debt expense	5,000
Total	405,000
Marginal income	295,000
Direct fixed expenses	
Salaries	30,000
Supplies	2,000
Telephone	600
Membership fees	500
Subscriptions	100
Advertising	1,000
Total	34,200
Loan contribution	$260,800

Figure 12-6

loans. Personnel costs, equipment costs, and most other costs of lending activities are fixed or semifixed expenses.

Figure 12-6 shows the computation of monthly contribution for a hypothetical loan department of a bank. The marginal income earned by the loan department for the month is computed by deducting the cost of the funds loaned and the bad debt expense from total interest earned. The cost of funds loaned is computed by using a weighted average of the cost of the various sources from which the funds are secured by the bank. This average cost is charged to the loan department as the standard cost of the money used by the loan department. The cost measures the approximate additional cost the bank will incur for each additional dollar loaned. It is analogous to the direct standard cost of a unit of product in a manufacturing firm, and a loan officer can determine the marginal income of the loan by comparing this cost with the lending rate he sets on a loan.

From the marginal income, direct fixed expenses are deducted to arrive at loan department contribution for the month. The fixed costs include only the costs that are directly traceable to the loan department. No allocations of cafeteria, employee relations, or executive management expenses are included in these amounts. The contribution from the loan department can be evaluated by bank management to determine whether it provides for an adequate bank profit, but a net income figure for the loan department is a meaningless number.

Contribution plans for the loan department can be developed in the same manner that contribution plans for the marketing department of a manufacturing firm are developed. A loan department begins its profit planning activities by developing an estimate of the contribution expected from the different types of loans. Figure 12-7 presents a contribution plan for the loan department of a bank that makes three types of loans. Since certain advertising programs are tailored to a specific group of lenders, some advertising costs are directly traceable to each of the three types of loan. The same is true of salaries and supplies. Various forms of cost–volume–profit analyses can be performed for different levels of advertising for the three types of loan to ascertain the most profitable level of expenditure for this expense. Once the contribution plan for the loan department is established, it becomes the standard against which the loan department performance is measured.

If the contribution plan in Figure 12-7 is adopted as the budget plan for the bank, departmental performance can be evaluated by comparing the actual results of loan department activities for the year with the proposed plan. Actual results for the 12 months appear in Figure 12-8, which gives the total dollars invested in the various types of loans and the actual

Loan Department Contribution Plan by Type of Loan
for 12 Months Ending December 31, 19xx

| | Total | Type of Loan | | |
		Installment	Commercial	Real Estate
Interest earned	$ 800,000	$ 150,000	$ 400,000	$ 250,000
Cost of funds loaned (4%)	325,000	40,000	160,000	125,000
Bad debt expense	5,000	2,000	2,000	1,000
Total	330,000	42,000	162,000	126,000
Marginal income	470,000	108,000	238,000	124,000
Direct fixed costs				
Advertising	17,000	10,000	4,000	3,000
Salaries	141,000	60,000	46,000	35,000
Supplies	1,800	1,000	400	400
Total	159,800	71,000	50,400	38,400
Loan contribution	310,200	37,000	187,600	85,600
Common fixed costs				
Salaries	42,000			
Supplies	6,000			
Telephone	11.000			
Membership fees	1,400			
Subscriptions	800			
Advertising	3,000			
Total	64,200			
Loan department contribution	246,000			
Loan rate		15%	10%	8%
Dollars loaned	$8,125,000	$1,000,000	$4,000,000	$3,125,000

Figure 12-7

197

Loan Department Contribution:
Actual Results for year ended December 31, 19xx

Loans outstanding for year	
Installment	$1,200,000
Commercial	4,400,000
Real estate	3,000,000
	$8,600,000
Interest earned	$ 870,000
Cost of funds loaned	344,000
Bad debt expense	6,000
Total	350,000
Marginal income	520,000
Direct fixed costs	
Salaries	180,000
Supplies	9,000
Telephone	12,000
Membership fees	1,300
Subscriptions	900
Advertising	20,000
Total	$ 223,200
Loan department contribution	$ 296,800

Figure 12-8

expenses charged to the loan department. These amounts, together with the data from the budget plan in Figure 12-7, are used to construct the contribution report work sheet presented in Figure 12-9. This work sheet is the same form as that used in Chapter 7 to develop a contribution performance report for the marketing segments of a manufacturing company.

In this work sheet the amount of dollars loaned becomes the volume measure, instead of the number of units sold. Thus the actual dollar volume of the various loans is used to compute the numbers in the "Control Budget" column. Other data in the work sheet are computed just like those in the work sheets discussed in Chapter 7. The report that is based on this work sheet (Figure 12-10) gives the bank management an idea of how close the loan department contribution is to the planned amount, and it points out why the loan department missed its target. In Figure 12-10, for instance, bank managers can immediately see that $35,250 of the increased contribution came from a higher volume of dollars loaned to customers and that $5,190 of the added contribution came from a more profitable mix of loans. They can also see that higher interest rates on the loans resulted in an additional $10,000 of contribution.

Contribution Report Work Sheet for Year Ended December 31, 19xx

	Budget Plan	Control Budget	Actual Results	Variances Volume/ Mix	Variances Rate/ Cost
Interest earned	$800,000	$860,000	$870,000	$60,000	$10,000
Cost of funds loaned	325,000	344,000	344,000	(19,000)	–0–
Bad debt expense	5,000	5,560	6,000	(560)	(440)
Total	330,000	349,560	350,000	(19,560)	(440)
Marginal income	470,000	510,440	520,000	40,440	9,560
Marginal income percentage	.587500	.593535			
Direct fixed costs					
Salaries	183,000	183,000	180,000	–0–	3,000
Supplies	7,800	7,800	9,000	–0–	(1,200)
Telephone	11,000	11,000	12,000	–0–	(1,000)
Membership fees	1,400	1,400	1,300	–0–	100
Subscriptions	800	800	900	–0–	(100)
Advertising	20,000	20,000	20,000	–0–	–0–
Total	224,000	224,000	223,200	–0–	800
Loan department contribution	$246,000	$286,440	$296,800	$40,440	$10,360

Figure 12-9

Loan Department Contribution Report for Year Ended December 31, 19xx

Planned contribution		$246,000
Volume variance: increase in contribution because of		
added loan volume (.587500 × $60,000)		35,250
Mix variance		5,190
Standard contribution for actual dollars loaned		$286,440
Rate variance: increase in interest earned because of		
higher rates		10,000
Cost variances		
Variable costs, bad debts		(440)
Fixed costs		
Salaries	$3,000	
Supplies	(1,200)	
Telephone	(1,000)	
Membership fees	100	
Subscriptions	(100)	
Advertising	-0-	800
Actual loan department contribution		$296,800

Figure 12-10

The standard cost of funds used to compute the contribution variances in this report is adequate for evaluating loan department performance, but it does not furnish relevant information for pricing loans. This problem is corrected by providing daily or weekly information to loan officers on the current and projected cost of funds. These data supply current cost information that can be used by the loan officers in arriving at pricing decisions. However, since the standard cost remains the same throughout the reporting period, the factors that are directly affected by the loan officer's decisions (the variances in the performance report) are the only factors used to evaluate loan officer performance. But the current data on cost of funds provide the loan officers with the information needed for effective pricing decisions.

Another factor that can be included in the performance report is the earnings received by the bank from compensating balances. The loan officer who negotiates a compensating balance arrangement with a lender increases the lendable funds of the bank, which increases the bank earnings. Since the loan officer affects the amount of the compensating balance with the decisions he makes, his performance report should reflect the impact of the compensating balances he acquires for the bank. This component can be readily included in the performance report by adding to the loan department contribution an amount that reflects the added earnings from the compensating balance. In other words, the loan department performance report prepared by the accountant should include all factors affected by decisions made in the loan department which have an economic impact on the bank.

In summary, service businesses can benefit from the use of direct cost and contribution data as much as manufacturing businesses can. In the service business the primary emphasis of the cost control system is on the planning and control of semifixed expenses. Also, the identification of semifixed cost behavior patterns and the volume levels at which the costs move up or down is critical because such an identification allows incremental costs of decision alternatives to be readily identified. Contribution reports and analyses in service businesses are similar to those used in manufacturing businesses. The primary difference between the contribution reports in the two types of business lies in the relatively insignificant amount of variable cost that appears in the service company contribution report.

CHAPTER 13

MANAGEMENT ACCOUNTING AND HUMAN BEHAVIOR

Because people make the decisions that cause costs and revenues to go up and down, this chapter explores some of the ways in which people react to and are affected by the management accounting system. The accounting process is examined as a behavioral process, and some practical schemes for making accounting reports work effectively are presented.

ACCOUNTING AS A BEHAVIORAL PROCESS

Management accounting serves two broad functions: It provides information that permits a company to "keep track of things," and it provides information for decision making.* Information for decision making is heavily concerned with influencing the behavior of the recipient of that information. The budget report prepared for a department supervisor is intended to provide information for that individual's decisions, but the accountant has a clear notion of the action he wants the department supervisor to initiate if the budget report contains significant unfavorable cost variances. The accountant wants the budget report to stimulate the department supervisor to take steps to reduce the excessive costs being incurred in his department.

Consequently, the data included in the report, the report format, and the timing of report issuance all must be designed to cause the report recipient to take the action desired by the report preparer. The accountant cannot say that his job is merely to report the facts, because the facts he reports and the way he reports them determine the actions that company managers

* Edwin H. Caplan, *Management Accounting and Behavioral Science*, (Reading, Mass: Addison-Wesley, 1971).

202

will take. Consequently, the accountant must consider the recipient action he wants to evoke before he can design an effective accounting report.

To provide a framework for examining the role of management accounting in affecting human behavior, let us now review the components of the communication process. Figure 13-1 is a pictorial representation of the basic elements of the communication process.* Obviously, communication begins with a source—a person or group of persons who want to engage in communication. The purpose of the source is translated into a message, and the message is carried by a channel to a receiver. In an accounting setting, the accountant is the source, his message is the accounting information about costs (or revenues), the channel is usually the printed report, and the receiver is the department supervisor who gets the report. Each of these elements in the communication process is explored in more detail in the following paragraphs.

The source is the person who wants to communicate a message to a receiver; therefore, the source chooses what it is that he wants to communicate. This area becomes very important in a management accounting system because numerous changes are taking place inside and outside the business which are important to the decisions that managers make. Since it is impossible for the accountant to include in his system information about all the changes that are occurring, he chooses certain information about selected changes for inclusion in his accounting system. Thus the accountant limits the messages he wants to communicate to those that relate to the factors he has decided to include in his accounting information system. The messages that provide information for many management decisions will come from sources other than the accountant. This complicates the accounting process because the recipient action desired by the accountant when he prepares a report may not be elicited at the proper time—not because of a bad accounting report, but because messages the manager has received from nonaccounting sources cause him to act different from the way the accountant had intended.

Figure 13-1   The communication process.

* David K. Berlo, *The Process of Communication* (New York: Holt, Rinehart, & Winston, 1960). This book has a comprehensive discussion of the communication process, and it is a delight to read. The ideas on the communication process in this chapter are adapted from Berlo's book.

Several other factors influence the effectiveness with which the message produces the desired response in the receiver. The communication skills of the source, for instance, determine whether the receiver is able to decode the message he receives. If the source uses a great deal of jargon in constructing his message, the receiver may be unable to ascertain what action the source wants him to take. If an accountant composes a report primarily in highly technical accounting language, the department head who receives the report may be unable to respond in the manner that the accountant intended; simply because he can't understand the report well enough to determine what the accountant wants him to do.

The attitude of the source toward the receiver will also affect the effectiveness of the communication. The more favorable the attitude of the source toward the receiver, the more effective the communication. If an accountant feels that the department supervisors are lazy, ignorant, and incompetent, his accounting reports for them will be almost completely ineffective—his attitude will cause the supervisors to react negatively to any message he prepares, regardless of the message content. On the other hand, the supervisors will be much more likely to consider the accountant's messages seriously if they feel that he likes them and is interested in helping them do a good job.

Chris Argyris, one of the early writers on the subject of the impact of accounting on people, found numerous instances in which budget reports were not producing the desired response because the accountants considered the reports to be devices for finding fault.* Naturally, a manager is going to react negatively to an accountant's message if he knows the accountant is trying to make him look bad.

Message construction is an important factor in effective communication also, and there are three important factors in each message—the message code, the message content, and the message treatment. The message code refers to the vocabulary that is used to construct the message, together with the set of rules or procedures for combining the words of the vocabulary. The accounting discipline has its own vocabulary, and accountants follow certain procedures and rules in using this vocabulary.

Message content refers to the material in the message selected by a source to express his purpose. The accounts included in a report and the use (or lack of use) of comparative amounts determine the message content of an accounting report.

The amount of detail in the report, the arrangement of the data on the page, the sequence of data on the report, and similar factors refer to the component called message treatment. One of the most important de-

* Chris Argyris, "Human Problems with Budgets," *Harvard Business Review* (January–February 1953), p. 104.

terminants of message treatment is the receiver. The source communicates because he wants to induce the receiver to do something, and the source must compose his message in such a manner that the receiver will perform the action intended by the message source. The source chooses a code that is comprehensible to the receiver; he arranges the elements of the code in a manner that permits the receiver to understand the message with a minimum of effort; and he tries to formulate a message that will achieve the greatest possible impact on the receiver. That is, he constructs a message that causes the receiver to do what he, the source, intended to be done. Thus the content and arrangement of accounting reports must be tailored to fit the report recipient, motivating him to perform the actions desired by the accountant.

The communication channel refers to the medium that serves to carry the message from the source to the receiver. The printed page is used for many accounting reports, although verbal presentations of financial data with various visual depictions of the data are also used. Cathode-ray tubes are employed in some computerized systems for transmitting data to the receiver. As in message treatment, the channel used for transmitting the message should be the one that causes the receiver to take the action desired by the source.

The last link in the communication process is the receiver. He is the most important element in the whole process because if he does not perform in the manner intended by the source, communication has not taken place; and the source might as well be talking to himself. The accountant who is unable to induce supervisors to take the actions indicated by his reports could prepare no report and get the same result.

Because of the importance of the receiver in the communication process, the accountant must prepare reports that fit that individual. The language used in the report, the amount of detail, the channel used to carry the message, all must be chosen with the receiver in mind. The accountant does not send a 200-page computer printout to the president, nor does he provide sales information to a department supervisor in the factory. He selects the information that is suited to his receiver, and ideally, he treats the message in such a way that the receiver will respond in the desired manner. Each report, then, is tailored to fit the requirements of the decision maker to whom it is addressed.

The skill level of the receiver has an impact on the message constructed by the source. The greater the receiver's familiarity with the message code used by the source, the more sophisticated the message can be. For instance, an accountant can prepare much more elaborate accounting analyses for a manager who early in his career worked as an accountant than for a manager who has never studied accounting at all. The department supervisor who has never before received a flexible budget report will be much more likely to misinterpret the message in the report than the supervisor who has used such reports for several years.

Because of the importance of matching the accounting report to the skill level of the recipient, the accountant should choose one of the following approaches to the problem of communicating with unskilled managers: he can develop his reports by carefully selecting words and ideas that are familiar to the unskilled manager, or he can attempt to increase the skill level of the manager who receives the reports. The accountant who decides to match his reports to the unskilled managers may find that he cannot prepare the many different reports required without excessive cost. Accordingly, he may try to upgrade the accounting skills of the managers to a point that allows him to use a few different reports to serve all managers. In other words, if an existing report does not fit a manager's skills, the report can be changed or the manager's skills can be changed to make the two factors more congruent.

THE MEANING OF MEANING

Because an important ingredient of the communication process is meaning, this concept is explored to determine its usefulness to the management accounting process. An accountant who prepares an analysis of a make-or-buy decision knows what the results mean, but the manager who receives the analysis may not know what that analysis means. The meaning of the budget reports the accountant prepares for a department supervisor is clear to the accountant, but it may be unclear to the department supervisor. Or, as another illustration, consider the number of discussions that take place in a company about the meaning of a given word or group of words. In each case meaning is important, but what does "meaning" mean? Can it be transferred from one person to another?

First of all, meanings are in people, not in words, dictionaries, or encyclopedias. Meanings are responses contained within the individual. The individual can learn or forget meanings, but he cannot find them. People who associate the same, or similar, meanings with a group of words can readily communicate with one another. Accountants can communicate with one another because most accountants attach the same meaning to the technical words used in accounting. The more a manager has studied accounting, the more closely will his meaning of accounting terms correspond to that of company accountants; and the more closely his meanings correspond to those of the accountants, the more readily he can communicate with them.

Since meanings are in people rather than words, communication does not consist of the transfer of meaning from the source to the receiver. The accounting report that is sent to the department supervisor does not carry meaning to the supervisor. It evokes meanings that are already present in the supervisor's mind, but it does not transmit any meaning to him. If the reports he prepares are to cause the desired response in the receiver, the accountant must be sure that both he and the recipient attach the same meaning to the content of the report. Otherwise, the response desired by the accountant will not be forthcoming.

Many people (even some accountants) feel that meanings are in words and numbers. The accountant who argues that the report he sends to a department head presents the facts is acting as if meanings are in words and not in people. So is the manager who sends memos to his subordinates and then complains that they don't do what they are told. Any individual in the company who explains a problem he is having with an employee by saying "I told him how to do the job, but he did it wrong anyway," is assuming that meanings are in words and not in people. Because of the disruptive effect on effective communication of the assumption that meaning is in words, the accountant should be careful to avoid making this assumption in his dealings with company managers.

HUMAN MOTIVATION

The actions that a manager takes when he receives an accounting report are dependent not only on how well the accountant has constructed his message but also on the motivational scheme used by company managers. To provide some insights into the complexities of human motivation, three of the more popular ideas are now reviewed. An examination of Maslow's need hierarchy is followed by a summary of Herzberg's "motivation-hygiene" factors. Finally, McGregor's "theory X" and "theory Y" are considered.

Abraham Maslow* developed an explanation of motivation based on five levels of basic needs: physiological, safety, love and belongingness, esteem, and self-actualization. The *physiological* or bodily need includes the need for food, clothing, and shelter. This need is a strong motivating factor when, for example, an individual lacks sufficient income to adequately feed and clothe himself. As this need becomes satisfied, however, its ability to motivate declines and the next need in the hierarchy, *safety*, becomes important.

* Abraham H. Maslow, *Motivation and Personality* (New York: Harper & Row, 1954).

Safety refers to the need an individual has to protect himself from unexpected events. For instance, a manager who is working for a company that has just been purchased by another company may feel insecure about his future job prospects. Because this need for safety is stimulated, he may take various actions designed to protect his job rather than concentrating on doing the job well.

As the safety and physiological needs are satisfied, the need for *love and belongingness* begins to become an important motivator. This is an individual's need to feel that he is part of a group, that his coworkers accept him as part of the group. As an illustration of frustration of this need, consider the case of an employee who displeases his fellow workers and who is then completely ignored by them. Only an extremely strong individual can function for long in this type of environment. Ultimately the ostracized employee will conform to the group desires, or he will quit his job.

If the first three needs are satisfied, the fourth need, *esteem*, becomes a strong motivating factor. Esteem refers to the self-respect an individual has and to the respect he receives from others. This need is satisfied when a person feels that what he is doing is worthwhile and important; it can easily be unfilled in an employee whose boss constantly criticizes his work and does not allow the employee to exercise initiative in performing his work. An employee in the latter circumstance will be unhappy in his work even though he is extremely well paid.

Self-actualization is the final need, and it concerns the need that an individual has to feel that the work he is doing is a creative expression of his potential. The individual who finds his work gratifying and who feels his work requires creativity is satisified with respect to the need for self-actualization.

The five needs are listed hierarchically in Figure 13-2. Usually, as the needs at one level are satisfied, the individual's desires shift to the next level. However, motivating an individual is not simply a matter of satisfying one need at a time. Rather, several needs are satisfied in various degrees; and as needs at one level become partially satisfied, needs at a higher level become more important as motivating factors. Also, some individuals have much stronger needs for esteem and self-actualization than do others. Interestingly, this approach to human motivation prescribes nonfinancial rewards for motivating the employee who is already earning an adequate salary. In other words, if an employee is earning an adequate salary, he can be motivated to increase his work output by rewarding his higher-level needs—and this costs the company nothing.

Frederick Herzberg's approach to the study of motivation differs from Maslow's. Herzberg cites what he calls "motivation" and "hygiene" factors to explain what induces people to perform.* He developed these two factors from an investigation in which he asked individuals to describe job experiences during which they had felt "exceptionally good" or "exceptionally bad" about their jobs. His study showed that most favorable experiences were related to attributes of the job content. The job attributes that most people liked were related to the top needs (esteem and self-actualization) in Maslow's hierarchy. That is, the people who were studied found their satisfaction in achievement, recognition, responsibility, and advancement. Herzberg classified these factors as motivators, because their presence seemed to motivate workers to high productivity.

On the other hand, the characteristics that his subjects found unfavorable related to the context of the job. Things such as company policies, supervision, pay, job status, and job security were frequently described as elements in job dissatisfaction. These dissatisfiers were classified by Herzberg as hygiene factors; that is, factors that lead to decreased output.

In attempting to understand Herzberg's approach, it is important to realize that the motivation and hygiene factors are not opposite ends of a scale but are two separate scales. The presence of motivation factors positively motivates an individual to high performance, but the lack of motivators does not mean that the employee is dissatisfied; it simply means that he is not motivated. On the other hand, an employee who has good working conditions, high pay, and job security, may not be motivated to high performance. The presence of such conditions (high pay, etc.) means that the job dissatisfiers have been removed; but in the absence of motivators,

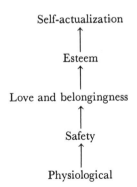

Figure 13-2   Maslow's hierarchy of needs.

* Frederick Herzberg, Bernard Mausner, and Barbara Synderman, *The Motivation to Work* (New York: Wiley, 1959).

the employee is not stimulated to high performance. The optimal condition for high performance (using Herzberg's approach) is one in which negative hygiene factors are eliminated and positive motivators are added to the job.

Still another approach to human behavior and motivation focusing on how managers assume employees behave is that developed by Douglas McGregor.* His two theories that explain how people behave—"theory X" and "theory Y"—concern the assumptions that managers make about how their employees are motivated.

The assumptions about how people behave that are included in theory X are as follows.

1. Employees strongly dislike work and will avoid it whenever possible.

2. Because they dislike work, employees will strive toward an organization goal only when they are very carefully controlled and know they will be severely punished if they deviate from the plan they are supposed to follow.

3. Individuals want security, they want to avoid responsibility, they lack ambition, and they want to be told exactly what to do.

Although these assumptions are contrary to both Maslow's and Herzberg's ideas on motivation, the environment in which an individual works may cause him to react the way theory X assumes he will act. For example, an employee who has a well-paying job that requires no initiative, a supervisor who is quick to point out what the employee does wrong, and so on, may feel that work is unpleasant. Furthermore, because the boss always points out the employee's mistakes, the latter will be extremely reluctant to take on any responsibility or to do anything he is not specifically told to do. Consequently, his job environment may cause him to display all the characteristics of theory X, not because the employee inherently possesses these characteristics but because the job causes the employee to display these attributes.

Theory Y, on the other hand, refers to a different set of assumptions about how people behave. These assumptions are:

1. Expenditure of effort in working is as natural as rest or play.

2. If an individual is committed to a certain goal, he will exercise self-direction and control to attain that goal.

3. The individual's commmitment to an objective is related to the rewards associated with the achievement of that objective.

4. Individuals not only learn to accept responsibility, they seek out the responsibility in the proper environment.

* Douglas D. McGregor, *The Human Side of Enterprise* (New York: McGraw-Hill, 1960).

5. Large segments of workers have the imagination, the ingenuity, and the creativity to solve organizational problems.

These assumptions, of course, run counter to the rather popular notion that a boss is a boss is a boss . . . . However, when the limitations of authority are considered, the theory Y assumptions do not appear to be so unrealistic. For example, few managers are able to fire an employee whenever they feel like doing so; and the greater the pressure managers exert to get employes to work harder, the greater the counterpressure generated by the employees. Furthermore, a foolproof system for planning and controlling employee activities cannot be devised unless the employees are willing to cooperate with the system. Thus the theory Y assumptions do provide a reasonable basis for looking at organizational behavior in some cases.

The motivational scheme used in an organization will affect the ability of the accountant to produce the receiver actions he wants with his accounting reports. For example, consider a company in which the managers use the theory X assumptions about human behavior, focus their attention on satisfying the lower-level needs in Maslow's hierarchy, and try to provide most of Herzberg's hygiene factors. In this kind of environment, the accountant will probably have difficulty getting the behavior he wants with his reports. The report receiver will probably look on the report as a device that is used to make him look bad, and he will probably scrutinize the report with care to see whether he can place the blame for any unfavorable budget variances on somebody else. Moreover, because the managers in this case assume that the workers are lazy, it is likely that unfavorable budget variances will be attributed to a lack of employee diligence on the job.

This kind of environment will cause the people who receive the reports to resort to all types of schemes to make themselves look good on their reports. Figure fudging, lowered quality, and production jams are just a few of the problems that budget reports can cause in this type of management environment.* Thus the accountant may intend a report noting unfavorable budget variances to stimulate cost-cutting activities, but instead the report may cause its recipient to devote a great deal of time trying to blame another manager for the unfavorable variances; and time spent in trying to place blame for variances is time wasted.

On the other hand, consider an environment in which managers use the

* Frank J. Jasinski, "Use and Misuse of Efficiency Controls," *Harvard Business Review* (July–August 1956), pp. 105–112. This article lists a number of instances in which the action intended by the report preparer was much different from the action taken by the report receiver.

theory Y assumptions about human behavior, focus their attention on satisfying the higher level needs in Maslow's hierarchy, and try to provide most of Herzberg's motivators. In this management environment the accountant is usually able to use his reports to stimulate the action he wants. Managers tend to use the accounting reports to point out areas in which questions should be asked, rather than using the information to place blame. The report recipient will tend to view the accounting reports as instruments that help him do better work, instead of showing where his performance is deficient. Since employees are given a great deal of responsibility in this type of environment, the accounting report will also inform the manager directly on how well he is doing his job.

These two examples of the management environment and the ability of the accountant to get the action he wants from his reports point out that the management environment does have an impact on the effectiveness of such reports. Consequently, to maximize the effectiveness of his reports, the accountant must take his environment into account when he designs his accounting system.

HUMAN BEHAVIOR AND ACCOUNTING REPORT DESIGN

Report design must consider the report recipients if the reports are to be effective. As noted earlier in the chapter, the objective of a message is to influence the actions of the person who receives the message; and the recipient is influenced in the way the source intended if he understands the message and if the proper management environment is present. Thus, the accounting report must be tailored to fit the individual receiving the report, or the accountant cannot reasonably expect him to respond in the desired manner.

The first step in designing a report is to determine what managerial decisions can benefit from accounting information. A position description will furnish some idea of the decision making authority possessed by a specific manager, but it should be used only as a starting point. Discussions with the manager about the kinds of accounting information he wants will yield additional information about the decisions he makes. During these discussions the accountant should also suggest types of accounting information that seem to be appropriate for the manager, for this will stimulate the manager to consider information that he may not have known he could draw on. In this stage of report design, then, the accountant and the manager attempt to identify the decisions made by the manager that will benefit from accounting information.

Next the accountant and the manager prepare crude decision models for the various decisions to determine how the manager expects to react to different accounting information. For instance, a decision model will be formulated to describe what actions a manager will take if there is an unfavorable (or favorable) material usage variance in his department. The size of variance necessary before action is taken is identified, and the speed with which action is taken for different variance amounts is also established. The optimum time lag between the occurrence of an event and the report of that event to the manager should also be agreed on by the accountant and the manager. The information collected by the accountant in these interviews serves as a foundation for the next step in designing the report— namely, formulating a statement of the recipient behavior desired from the various messages that the accountant can send to the manager. Of course, the desired behavior will be the behavior the manager has indicated he will take when he receives a given message. The accountant does not gather the information about decisions and decision models to be able to manipulate the manager's actions; rather, his aim is to induce the manager to do what the manager has said he will do on receipt of a given message.

Following this statement of desired behavior, the accountant selects the appropriate medium to carry his messages to the manager. Should the accountant put all his messages in one monthly report, or should he use several different reports? Should he use voice communication for some messages, or should all messages be written on pieces of paper? The answers to these questions depend on the type of action the accountant desires from the message recipient. If he wants an instantaneous response, he may transmit the the message by voice (in person or by telephone); if he is willing to accept a delayed response, he may transmit the message in writing; and if he expects a series of actions spread over a certain time span, he will probably use a form of document that can be referred to by the recipient during the period under consideration. The medium selected for transmitting the message to the manager is determined by the response desired from the message recipient.

Following the selection of the medium to be used to transmit the message, the accountant next constructs the message to be carried. That is, he chooses the terminology, the format, the level of detail, the sequence of data, and so on, that will enable the receiver to efficiently attach to the message the meaning intended by the accountant. Consider the two reports shown in Figure 13-3. These reports were prepared from the same underlying data, yet the first report uses 14 lines of data and the second uses only 6 lines. Figure 13-3b identifies specific expense variances only if they exceed $225, whereas Figure 13-3a identifies budget amounts, actual

The XYZ Company
Performance Report

Department: Machining
Supervisor: R. Jones
Period: July

	Standard	Actual	Variance	Achievement (%)
Materials	$45,600	$45,900	($300)	99
Labor				
Rate	7,800	8,000	(200)	98
Efficiency	7,600	7,800	(200)	98
Overhead				
Efficiency	3,260	3,320	(60)	98
Spending	3,320	3,065	255	107
	$67,580	$68,085	($505)	

	Standard	Actual	Variance	Achievement (%)
Overhead expense spending				
Supervision	$ 400	$ 430	($30)	93
Material handling	315	330	(15)	95
Operating supplies	1,248	1,000	248	125
Spoilage	312	320	(8)	98
Depreciation, taxes, and insurance	420	420	0	100
Power	225	215	10	105
Maintenance	400	350	50	114
	$ 3,320	$ 3,065	$255	

Figure 13-3a   Message construction, example I.

amounts, and variances. The action desired by the accountant is different for each report.

The lengthy report may be used to induce the recipient to praise the accountant for his ability to compute the difference between budget and actual amounts and for his ability to correctly total a column of figures; but any desire of the accountant to motivate the supervisor to reduce expenses is clouded by the mass of numbers. However, the short report shows the items the supervisor originally indicated he considers to be important, and nothing more. Compared with the first report, the meaning the accountant attaches to the second document is much more likely to be the same as that used by the supervisor. The accountant may also provide the supervisor with the detail shown in the more elaborate report, permitting the supervisor to refer to it during the month to answer questions about his department. In this case the accountant uses the detailed report as a data file for the department supervisor rather than as a means of inducing action.

If the manager wants a brief report that identifies all major variances but omits the detail shown in Figure 13-3a, the accountant can prepare a report like that in Figure 13-4. This report lists the standard amount and the variance; the amounts appear in variance amount sequence, starting with the largest variance. If this procedure is consistently followed, the supervisor will know that the largest variance is always first and that smaller ones are listed later. Thus the variance at the top of the report is usually the one requiring immediate action and the others are less urgent. Obviously, the manager could glean this informtion from a longer report, but there should be no need for him to go to this trouble if the accountant is doing his job.

The XYZ Company
Variance Report

Department: Machining
Period: July

Item		Amount
Material usage		($300)
Overhead spending		
Operating supplies	$248	
Other overhead items	7	255
Other variances		(460)
Total departmental variance		($505)

Figure 13-3b   Message construction, example II.

XYZ Company
Performance Report

Department: Machining
Period: July

	Standard	Variance	Achievement (%)
Material usage	$45,600	($300)	99
Labor efficiency	7,600	(200)	98
Labor rate	7,800	(200)	98
Overhead efficiency	3,260	(60)	98
Overhead spending	3,320	255	108
Total		($505)	

Figure 13-4

Because reports are tailored to fit people and because people are changeable creatures, the reports used by a company should be periodically reviewed to see that they are accomplishing what the accountant wants them to accomplish. Each report should be reevaluated at least once a year, or whenever a manager is replaced. Reports that were suitable for one manager are not necessarily appropriate for his successor; therefore, the new manager should be interviewed as soon as possible after he assumes his new post to ensure that the reports he receives will produce the actions desired by the accountant.

In summary, the design of an effective accounting report is a complex process that involves a great deal of interaction between the accountant and the managers who use accounting reports. The accountant must attempt to identify the decisions the manager makes that benefit from accounting information, establish how these decisions are made, and construct messages that stimulate the appropriate actions on the part of the managers receiving the reports.

CHAPTER 14

INSTALLING A DIRECT COST SYSTEM

The amount of difficulty encountered in installing a direct cost and contribution reporting system varies inversely with the sophistication of the existing system. A company with a well-defined departmental structure, a detailed chart of accounts, and a clearly defined organization will have little difficulty converting to direct costing. The company with none of these features will have to do a lot of preparatory work before a direct cost system can be installed. The first part of the discussion in this chapter is based on the assumption that the company has no detailed chart of accounts, departmental structure, or organization chart. The reader who already has these elements functioning smoothly in his company can skip to the paragraphs that deal with cost behavior analysis. The chapter closes with a consideration of the various ways of adjusting direct costs to conform to external reporting requirements.

GETTING READY FOR DIRECT COSTING

For the company that is starting from scratch to develop a management accounting system based on direct cost and contribution data, one of the best methods of beginning the collection and organization of information involves the use of a work flow diagram—a flow chart of the activities that are performed to manufacture the company's product. The flow chart in Figure 14-1, for example, shows the production activities involved in producing wine. Each block on this chart represents a group of activities that are performed to manufacture the finished product; grape receiving activities are represented by the first block, grape inspection activities by the second block, and so forth. The arrows indicate the product flow from

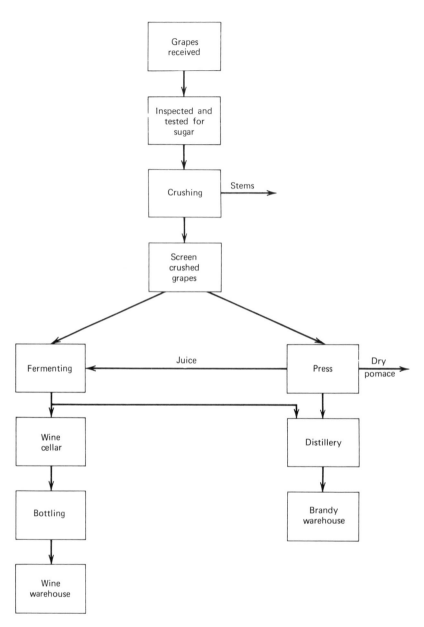

Figure 14-1

one group of activities to another. This flow chart of processing activities for wine production illustrates how the various production activities are diagrammed for a continuous processing activity; however, if products are custom made to customer specifications, a simple flow diagram such as that in Figure 14-1 cannot be drawn, because every product requires a different set of activities.

In custom product companies, a diagram of the activities that can be performed on the various products is drawn without lines indicating possible product flow. The accountant who develops this type of diagram uses it to focus his attention on the activities that can be performed in his company's plant. In developing such a diagram, the accountant constantly

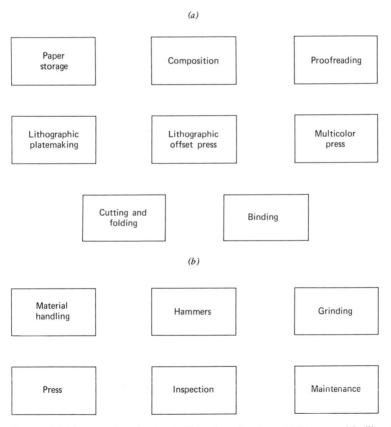

Figure 14-2   (*a*) Diagram of production facilities for print shop. (*b*) Diagram of facility producing forgings.

asks himself what kinds of activities the company can perform on a product. By answering this question, he identifies the activities the enterprise can perform to complete the work required by its customers. Figure 14-2a, for instance, shows the groups of activities that can be performed in the typical print shop (doing composition work for customers, making lithographic plates for custom work, etc.). Each block in the diagram represents one activity or a group of activities that the print shop can perform for its customers. Figure 14-2b is a similar diagram for a forging facility that produces products to fit customer needs; it is prepared in the same way that the one for the print shop is developed.

After diagramming the work flow or the activity centers, the accountant sets out to identify departments and cost centers. This procedure consists of grouping the activities represented by the blocks in the work flow diagram into units that are large enough to make up a production or service department. Some activities may be significant enough to make up a department without the addition of other activities; in other instances, a number of the blocks in the diagram are placed together in one department. The number of activities grouped in a department depends on how the company wants to organize its activities. Thus this stage of system development interfaces with the definition of organizational responsibilities that is essential to a smoothly functioning management accounting system. An organization chart must be prepared prior to or, at the latest, simultaneously with this stage of systems development.

Following the identification of production activities with organization segments, the accountant turns his attention to the preparation of a chart of accounts. The amount of detail included in this chart of accounts is dependent on the detail required by the individuals who will use the reports generated by the system. Consequently, interviews with department supervisors and plant managers provide the best source of information on the accounts to be included in the chart of accounts. Standard charts of account prepared by trade associations furnish a convenient starting point for a chart of accounts, but these accounts should never be used without a lengthy discussion of their suitability with company managers at all levels.

The same holds true for the existing chart of accounts in use by the company—it should not be continued under the new direct cost system until it has been thoroughly reviewed.* The chart should be examined to determine whether the accounts and the account codes will permit the accumulation of data necesary for the production of direct cost and contribution reports

---

* John V. James, "Things Learned in the Installation of Direct Costing," *Management Accounting* (formerly *NAA Bulletin*) (March 1962), pp. 77–78.

by the new system. Account descriptions should be clear and concise, to ensure that all people in the company will be using the accounts consistently.

The reports to be generated by the system may be developed concurrently with the preparation of the chart of accounts, since the information included in the reports determines the data that are collected and summarized in the accounts. Report design, as noted in Chapter 13, is essentially a behavioral process in which the accountant selects the design and content that should elicit the desired behavior in the report recipient. As a result, the chart of accounts is affected by the report content that is needed to produce the behavior desired of the report recipient, and the comments in Chapter 13 about the human behavior side of accounting are relevant to the design of the chart of accounts.

Cost behavior analysis is the next step in the installation of a direct cost system. Companies that already have a detailed chart of accounts should encounter little difficulty in identifying the behavior patterns of the costs incurred in the various company segments. If the chart of accounts is inadequate, the company must review and update its chart of accounts before it can perform a satisfactory cost behavior analysis. The cost behavior analysis proceeds in the way described in Chapter 3: cost behavior patterns are identified, and then the dollar amounts of expenses are measured.

Out of this process, the data for direct material, labor, and overhead costs are developed. These data provide the information for the overhead rate and amount budget and for the material and labor standards. Step costs must be clearly identified in this process so costs are properly controlled. The following quotation shows how one company handled its semifixed expenses in its budget system.

To explain further our application of step budgets, with relatively simple analysis, base levels of spending were determined for each capacity cost department. Further, we recognized that significant changes in production would require additional expenditures for clerical and indirect labor, supplies, travel, etc. Depending upon the function or department, we were able to determine the amount of expense for each major production or activity level. These activity levels were based on shifts per day, days per week, or the number of production units operating. The budget for each step was then established to represent the amount of expense expected in these capacity-cost or overhead departments if operations were carried out at the particular level for a prolonged time period.*

* Marsall W. Webster, "Installing a New Direct Cost System," *Management Accounting* (formerly *NAA Bulletin*) (March 1971), pp. 31–33.

Service Department Costs

Production information
  Standard production rate: 60 units per machine hour
  Kilowatt-hours per machine hour: Department A = 65
  Kilowatt-hours per machine hour: Department B = 25
  Variable power department cost per kilowatt-hour: $.024805
Power cost per unit of product
  Department A (65 × .024805) ÷ 60 = .02687
  Department B (25 × .024805) ÷ 60 = .01034

Source: Adapted from Ray E. Longenecker "Converting to Direct Costing," *Management Accounting* (formerly *NAA Bulletin*) (August 1962), p. 32.

Figure 14-3

If absorption overhead budgets are currently being used by the company, these can be converted to direct cost budgets by separating the variable overhead expenses from the fixed ones and eliminating allocations of fixed expenses from other departments. In other words, converting from absorption overhead budgets to direct cost overhead budgets involves a simplification of the process of identifying overhead costs with departments and products.

Service department costs sometimes cause problems because of the difficulty of measuring the change in service department cost that is due to a change in the level of activity in a producing department. Consider power costs, for instance. Engineers can measure the amount of power that is used for each hour of machine time.* This amount can be converted to a dollar cost by multiplying the quantity of power used per machine hour by the variable cost of producing that power, and the results of this computation reveal the increase in company costs from operating the machine for one hour. Figure 14-3 shows how this approach can be used to develop the power cost direct to each unit of product. In this figure the machines can produce 60 units of product each hour. The machines in department A use 65 kWhr per machine hour, and the machines in department B use 25 kWhr per machine hour. The Kilowatt-hour usage of each machine is multiplied by the cost of $.024805/kWhr for the total power cost per machine hour. This amount is divided by the 60 units that can be produced per machine hour to arrive at the power cost direct to each unit of product

---

* Roy E. Longenecker, "Converting to Direct Costing," *Management Accounting* (formerly *NAA Bulletin*) (August 1962).

produced. In this way service department costs that are related to changes in production are made a part of the unit cost.

The service department costs that are constant regardless of the level of production are charged to the segment responsible for the cost. The cost of lighting the plant, which remains constant regardless of the level of production, is charged to the plant manager, since his decisions determine the level of the cost. Also, plant lighting is a semifixed expense, varying with the number of days the plant is open during the week. The budget for this portion of the power cost is a step budget, with different levels of costs for the number of days that the plant is open.

Clear identification of power cost with producing departments, products, and the plant, which permits the individuals who affect power costs with their decisions to see the cost effect of such decisions, is a necessary step for a company that is changing from absorption to direct costing. Of course, this presumes that power cost a significant cost of producing the product. But if power is a relatively insignificant cost, there will be other service department costs that must be identified just as power cost was derived in Figure 14-3. Maintenance cost, for example, must be related to production levels, production departments, and to segments that have plant-wide responsibility. In summary, converting to direct costing from absorption costing requires that the interrelationships among production activities and service department activities be clearly specified for product costing and for responsibility accounting.

CONVERTING TO DIRECT COSTING

Planning for the conversion from absorption to direct costing requires the same careful attention as any other major project undertaken by the company. Consequently, a company's first step in the conversion process should be to develop a timetable of activities. These activities are frequently placed on a network to show the interrelationships among the various activities and to identify the critical activities for completing the conversion on schedule. Included in this original plan will be such activities as revision of chart of accounts, cost behavior analysis, and overhead budget preparation.

Next, the people who will direct and carry out the installation of the conversion are selected. Usually a financial executive heads the task force assembled to install the system. The skills and numbers of the remaining members of the task force will depend on the scope of the conversion project. For example, if the company already has a well-developed absorption system with an extensive chart of accounts, the system can be implemented by a small team consisting of financial and procedures personnel. If the company is installing its first cost system as part of its conversion to direct costing, a larger and more diverse task force is needed. Since some of the skills used for installing the system will also be required to keep it operating, it may become necessary to hire added personnel to help with the installation. However, the company should attempt to hire only the number of personnel that will be needed to keep the system operating once it is installed. Otherwise the company may find that it has a top-heavy permanent staff with little to do after installation is completed. Securing the advice of outside consultants on selected problems is one way to obtain expertise without building up a large permanent staff.

Training company employees to use the new system is one of the major activities facing the task force. An extensive training program is required for most installations to acquaint company managers with the characteristics of direct costing. This training program can vary from an informal approach in which accountants talk to managers on an individual basis to a formal program of group training sessions. The informal approach works well if the number of managers to be trained is small, and it also is the most effective way to deal with lower level managers who are busy making day-to-day decisions. One company used the following approach to training its supervisory personnel:

We changed our report to a direct-cost basis, then had our accounting staff work with all levels of supervision to explain the changes we made and what we were trying to achieve. We solicited comments and suggestions on design of reports and furnished reference figures, such as gross margin, so that supervisory management could better understand the difference between direct-costing and whole-cost methods.*

However, such an informal approach to training may not be sufficient if it is necessary to train many supervisors and sales personnel to use the direct cost information. When a large number of managers must be familiarized with direct cost concepts and techniques, formal training programs are usually necessary. The task force in charge of training company personnel should prepare case studies and examples based on the actual conditions faced by the company managers in their work. The conversion of recent monthly or quarterly accounting reports to direct costing provides a means of showing how the direct cost reports differ from the absorption cost reports. Since conversion of absorption cost reports to direct cost is a relatively simple procedure, this method of demonstrating the difference

* James, *op. cit.,* p. 81.

between the old and the new reporting system is an easily used—and most effective—way of highlighting the differences between the two techniques.

It is frequently objected that if direct cost information is introduced into sales reports, sales personnel will start using such data to underprice the product. To guard against this eventuality, the training program for sales personnel should focus on the necessity of generating enough contribution to cover common costs and profits. The contribution generated by various salesmen and territories can be reconstructed for the past year to show the amounts generated in the past to cover common costs and profits. Cost–volume–profit techniques can be used to demonstrate how the sales personnel can evaluate the impact on their respective contributions of various selling prices. If the company does not use budgets, the training program can emphasize the importance of generating a contribution amount that at least equals that of past periods. If a budget system is used, the training program can focus on the importance to company profits of sales segments meeting their contribution targets. When sales and marketing personnel understand adequately the concept of contribution, underpricing of company products should not be a problem, especially if performance evaluation is based on the attainment of contribution targets.

So far this discussion has assumed that the accounting staff is adequately trained in the concepts and techniques of direct costing. This is seldom the case, however, since few textbooks adequately explain the practical application of direct cost techniques. To correct this problem, discussion sessions on direct costing can be held for the accounting staff, and several members of the staff might attend relevant seminars and courses to gain a working knowledge of the concept. The company may find that it is easier to explain the direct cost concepts to managers than it is to persuade the accountants to change their way of thinking. Managers tend to view the conversion to direct costing as the substitution of a technique that is understandable for one that is incomprehensible. On the other hand, accountants tend to view the implementation of direct costing techniques as a threat to their standard procedures. Many times accountants have devoted so much of their energy to searching for the "correct" way to allocate a cost that they find it difficult to believe that what has been so troublesome a problem is not really a problem at all. In any event, never underrate the importance of training the accounting staff in the use of direct costing techniques.

The conversion to direct costing also brings up the problem of deciding when to change the accounting records to the new system. Most companies swing over to the new system at the beginning of a new fiscal year, but this is usually done because it is convenient for top level reports. Companies can easily convert to direct costing at any time during the year because of

Steps Followed in Converting to a Direct Cost System

---

1. Appoint a task force to direct the conversion to direct cost.
2. Prepare work flow or activity center diagram.
3. Identify departments or cost centers.
4. Prepare detailed chart of accounts.
5. Design reports for the system.
6. Identify and measure fixed and variable portions of all expenses.
7. Train managers and accounts to work with system.

Figure 14-4

the ease of reconstructing direct cost reports to a prior base. Some companies with several plants in different geographic locations will convert one plant at a time to direct costing, with little attention to the beginning of the fiscal year.

In summary, conversion to direct cost and contribution reporting will proceed smoothly if it is carefully planned and controlled. The steps to be followed in the conversion to direct cost are summarized in Figure 14-4 for easy reference.

DIRECT COSTS AND EXTERNAL REPORTING

When the direct cost system is installed and operating, the company must face the problem of preparing external financial reports that conform to the rules of financial reporting. Since direct cost data are not acceptable for external reports, the company must add to the balance in the inventory account an amount that represents the fixed costs considered by external reporting rules to be a part of the inventory cost. This fixed cost amount can be carried in a separate account that is adjusted annually, or an adjusting entry can be made each year to record the fixed costs that are added to the inventory. The adjusting entry is immediately reversed to prevent any account balance from being carried in the ledger for inventory fixed costs, but the fixed costs do appear in the financial reports and tax returns. If the fixed costs are carried in the ledger throughout the year, they can be used in quarterly or monthly external reports. The difference between the fixed amount and the "theoretically" correct amount for any one month or quarter will be immaterial in most cases.

The accountant might choose to convert direct costs to absorption costs by examining the relationship of fixed costs to variable costs—for example, by computing the ratio between fixed factory overhead and the variable costs of production. This ratio is then multiplied by the ending balance of direct cost inventory value to arrive at the total fixed cost to include in the inventory value. In Figure 14-5, which illustrates how this procedure works, annual plant fixed costs amount to $711,000; the direct cost in ending inventory is $200,000; and, the balance in the inventory period cost account is

Adjusting Direct Inventory Costs for External Reporting

I. Basic data
   Annual plant fixed costs $711,000
   Direct product costs
      Product A $10
      Product B   12
      Product C   15
   Planned production at beginning of year
      Product A   10,000
      Product B   20,000
      Product C   30,000
   Total direct cost in ending inventory $200,000
   Balance in inventory period cost account $150,000

II. Fixed cost adjustment computation
   Total planned variable cost

	Units	Cost	Total
Product A	10,000	$10	100,000
Product B	20,000	12	240,000
Product C	30,000	15	450,000
			790,000

Fixed cost ratio

$$\frac{\text{total fixed cost}}{\text{total planned variable cost}} \frac{711,000}{790,000} \times 100 = 90\%$$

Fixed cost included in inventory for external reporting
   Total direct cost in ending inventory $200,000
   Fixed cost ratio   90%
   Fixed cost in ending inventory $180,000

III. Adjustment to period cost account
   Dr. inventory period cost account $30,000
      Cr. income summary $ 30,000

Figure 14-5

Adjusting Direct Inventory Costs for External
Reporting—Work In Process Iventory

I. Basic data
    Inventory costs at year end

Finished goods	$160,000
Work in process	
Department X	80,000
Department Y	40,000
Department Z	30,000
Total direct inventory costs	$310,000

II. Fixed cost adjustment

Total direct inventory cost	$310,000
Fixed cost ratio	90%
Fixed cost in ending inventory	$279,000

Figure 14-6

$150,000. The production that was planned for the year would have resulted in planned variable costs of $790,000.

The variable cost is based on the number of units that the company originally expected to produce; it is the same volume that would have been used for computing an overhead rate in an absorption cost system. Because the variable costs are based on planned capacity of the plant, the ratio of total variable manufacturing cost to total fixed manufacturing cost furnishes a reasonable estimate of the fixed cost related to each unit. This ratio in Figure 14-5 is 90%. Consequently, the total variable cost of $200,000 in ending inventory is multiplied by the ratio to compute the $180,000 of fixed cost that is said by external reporting rules to be a part of inventory cost.

The inventory period cost account must now be adjusted to this higher level, and this is accomplished by debiting the account for the additional $30,000 required to increase it to $180,000. Income summary is credited by a like amount. Thus, as the typical example illustrates, profits under absorption costing vary with inventory levels instead of with sales. If the company in this case did not carry a balance in its inventory period cost account, the full $180,000 would be debited to this account, with a reversing entry processed at the beginning of the next accounting period to remove the account balance.

Work in process inventories can be handled in the same manner as the finished goods. Assume that the fixed cost ratio from Figure 14-5 also holds true for the data in Figure 14-6. Here finished goods make up $160,000 of the $310,000 in inventory; the remaining $150,000 is work in process inventory. Nevertheless, as this example shows, the fixed cost to be included in inventory on the balance sheet is obtained by adding the two inventories and multiplying the total by the fixed cost ratio.

Most of the articles that have been written on the subject of direct cost have dealt with the arguments for or against the use of direct cost inventory values for balance sheets and income statements. The net result of this exchange of ideas is that the rules for computing inventory costs are now the same as they were before the direct cost concept became popular. The accountants who make the rules that govern external reporting are primarily concerned with the development of a rationalization of the status quo. Thus direct costs in external reports, since they violate the status quo of absorption costing, are considered to be an unwarranted evil from which owners and creditors must be protected. One can also speculate about the possibility that the increased complexity of an absorption cost system does little to reduce the fees charged for audits, thereby causing no undue pressure on accountants for a change in the status quo.

Regardless of what the external reporting requirements may say about direct costs, the accountant can use them in any manner he pleases for internal reports and analyses. Furthermore, a direct cost system provides useful information for both internal and external reports; but absorption cost data are useful *only* for external reporting. They are completely useless for decision making at any level in the company.

REFERENCES

1. LeDuc, Harold, A., "Converting to a Direct Cost System," *Management Accounting* (formerly *NAA Bulletin*) (May 1965), pp. 17–22.
2. Portman, Richard K., "Installing Direct Costing in One Division of a Company," *Management Accounting* (formerly *NAA Bulletin*) (June 1958), pp. 5–12.
3. Thorn, William A., "Converting from Conventional to Direct Standard Costs," *Management Accounting* (formerly *NAA Bulletin*) (April 1958), pp. 83–93.
4. Williams, Richard E., "Converting to a Direct Costing System, "*Management Accounting* (formerly *NAA Bulletin*) (January 1968), pp. 23–34.

CHAPTER 15

DIRECT COSTS: SOME PROBLEMS AND AN OVERVIEW

Direct cost and contribution accounting provide an integrated management accounting system for business enterprises. However, there are two problems involved in using this system, and these are explored in this chapter; specifically, we deal with curvilinear cost functions and semifixed cost behavior patterns. Following this discussion, we present an overview of the major ideas on which direct cost and contribution accounting are based, as a concise summary of the rationale for this accounting system.

CURVILINEAR COST FUNCTIONS

The cost behavior patterns discussed in Chapter 2 were illustrated using straight lines (see Figure 2-2), and throughout this book variable cost has been treated as though a straight line described its behavior. This assumption of linearity is usually justified by contending that within relatively narrow ranges of production, the variable costs will increase or decrease by a constant amount for each unit change in output. And this argument holds true for numerous variable and semivariable costs; but it is not an essential feature of direct costing. That is, direct cost accounting does not presume that all variable and semivariable costs change in a constant amount for each unit change in output.

Before the advent of widespread computer usage in accounting systems, the assumption of a linear cost relationship was probably important because of the possible difficulty of coping with curvilinear cost functions in a hand-posted system. With the current proliferation of computer programs in accounting practice, this justification for cost linearity in the system is no longer important. Furthermore, in his book published in 1962, Wilmer

Wright described how nonlinear cost behavior patterns could be incorporated into a direct cost system.*

The accounting system is more complex with the curvilinear cost functions than with the linear cost behavior patterns, but with a computerized system the complexity is at a manageable level. Figure 15-1a indicates how a curvilinear cost behavior pattern might be incorporated into a direct cost system. In this example the standard unit cost is $22, and this cost is incurred in three departments. The product costs are constant in all departments except in department 3, where labor cost per unit increases as daily production in that department exceeds 100 units. The unit cost curve Figure in 15-1b depicts the behavior of labor cost in this department, and the table in Figure 15-1a presents the same information. This pattern is exhibited because of the increasing inefficiency of labor as daily output exceeds 100 units and because higher wages must be paid for the overtime that is worked to produce the high output. Thus for department 3 the standard labor cost per unit is $3 for all daily production below 101 units, but it increases as production reaches and goes above that level.

A flexible type of standard cost is important for pricing products as the firm's output approaches capacity. If the firm produces the product to customer order, prices may have to be increased sharply as output in department 3 goes above 100 units per day. For example, assume that the product is normally sold for $28, that department 3 is producing 100 units per day, and that a customer wants to buy 100 units. This bloc of 100 units will cause daily production in department 3 to increase to 110 for 10 days (see Figure 15-2). As this figure shows, the marginal income from the sale of the additional 100 units is $241. If the standard cost of $22 had been used to compute the marginal income, the marginal income would have appeared to be $600, which is $359 above the actual marginal income earned from the order. Consequently, curvilinear cost behavior patterns should be incorporated into the direct cost system if the company expects to experience wide variations in output that cause unit costs to fluctuate. By instituting such a procedure, the company will have relevant unit cost data for all levels of production that fall within the range of expected production.

Not only are relevant unit cost data provided for pricing decisions, but cost data for planning and control decisions are also supplied by the system. The curvilinear cost behavior patterns will help to give more precise estimates of total costs as the planned production level approaches

* Wilmer Wright, *Direct Standard Costs for Decision Making and Control* (New York: McGraw-Hill, 1962). p. 41

I. Basic data
Product cost sheet

	Department			
	1	2	3	Total
Material	$4	$2	$3	$ 9
Labor	2	3	3	8
Overhead	2	1	2	5
Total	$8	$6	$8	$22

Units	Unit Cost	Cumulative Cost
First 100	3.00	300.00
101	3.10	303.10
102	3.15	306.25
103	3.20	309.45
104	3.30	312.75
105	3.40	316.15
106	3.55	319.70
107	3.70	323.40
108	3.90	327.30
109	4.15	331.45
110	4.45	335.90
111	4.85	340.75
112	5.35	346.10
113	6.00	352.10
114	6.90	359.00
115	8.00	367.00
116	9.50	376.50

Figure 15-1a   Curvilinear cost behavior patterns and direct cost systems.

II.   Unit cost curve

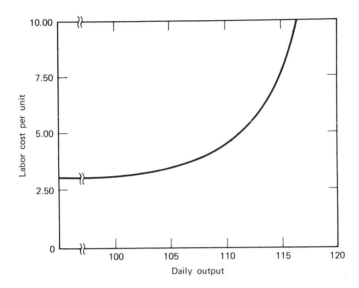

Figure 15-1*b*

the capacity of the plant. Cost control information will also be more precise than that based on linear cost behavior patterns because as output reaches capacity, the curvilinear standard cost increases more rapidly than the linear standard costs. Department supervisors will be freed from the necessity of explaining unfavorable cost variances that arise merely because the company is producing at a level near the plant capacity. In deciding whether to include curvilinear cost behavior patterns in the budgets and cost standards, the accountant must weigh the significance of the cost change. If a straight line is a reasonable approximation of a cost's behavior, there is no need to use a curvilinear pattern; however, if a straight line does not provide a reasonable approximation and if the dollar change is significant, the accountant should use a curvilinear cost behavior pattern.

The accountant does not have such flexibility in his treatment of semifixed costs. He may use a straight line to approximate semifixed cost behavior patterns only if the fixed cost increments are small and if they change for narrow changes in output. In all other cases the accountant must treat semifixed costs as semifixed costs. Because semifixed cost behavior patterns describe the behavior of numerous costs in the typical com-

Pricing Decisions and Curvilinear Cost Functions

I.	Basic data		
	Standard unit cost		$ 22
	Normal selling price		28
	Customer order		100 units
	Units produced		10 per day
II.	Analysis of order		
	Revenue		$2,800
	Variable costs		
	100 units × $22	$2,200	
	10 days × 35.90	359	2,559
			$ 241

Figure 15-2

pany, the direct cost system should incorporate these behavior patterns into the budgets and standards used by the company. Unfortunately, however, the increments in fixed cost do not appear in unit costs for semifixed cost behavior patterns, and as a result such increments may be overlooked when incremental costs are used for pricing decisions. To guard against this problem, the direct cost system should be designed to provide pricing managers with information about the change in total company costs for any change in output. That is, the system should furnish information about the variable cost changes as well as the semifixed cost changes brought about by the change in volume.

Because the budgets for the company segments already have semifixed expenses clearly identified, incremental costs for pricing decisions can be developed by giving the pricing manager a schedule of semifixed expenses for each company segment, as well as current information on production volume. Or, if the company has a computerized accounting system, this information can be stored in the computer and called forth by the pricing manager whenever he needs it. Consider the example in Figure 15-3, which presents the semifixed expense budgets for three production departments along with the standard cost of the unit produced. The standard cost, of course, includes only the variable costs of producing the product. The currently planned production for the coming month indicates that there is excess capacity in week 1 and in week 2. Consequently, when the company receives an offer for 400 units that can be produced during these two weeks, it is inclined to give the offer serious consideration.

When the standard cost of $28 is compared with the price of $30 offered for the units, the pricing manager might conclude that the offer should be accepted because of the $800 marginal income that would be generated. However, if he looks at the increase in semifixed costs that would be caused by the additional volume, he will notice that it completely offsets the marginal income, resulting in a $1,300 loss on the offer. Focusing exclusively on the marginal income in this case would have caused the pricing manager to accept an unprofitable offer; but by considering the impact on total company costs, he could evaluate the profit impact of accepting the offer. Such evaluations are relatively easy to make in a company that has a direct cost system; and the accountant should make sure that these analyses are facilitated by channeling information about semifixed costs to the pricing managers, who can make rational pricing decisions based on the changes in total company cost.

DIRECT COSTING: AN OVERVIEW

The idea that costs can be identified by their behavior patterns is essential to direct cost accounting. That is, every cost incurred by the business is analyzed to determine whether it varies with output and to determine how much it varies with output. These costs usually fall into variable, semivariable, and semifixed categories, and budgets are developed to reflect these behavior patterns. Fixed costs are also identified and incorporated into the budget system.

Segregation of costs by behavior pattern enables company managers to compute the changes in total company costs for any change in business activity and to use this information in their planning decisions. The alternative costs of producing various product mixes are readily available, as are the costs of operating company plants at varying levels of capacity. Cost control is also greatly enhanced with a direct cost system because of the ease with which the budgeted amount of cost for a given production volume can be computed. Because the costs are categorized by behavior pattern, it is a simple matter for the accountant to apply the actual level of production to the nonfixed expenses to compute the total of these expenses; he can add the fixed costs to the amount thus generated for the total budgeted expenses. No problems of over-or under absorbed overhead are encountered, nor does the accountant need to explain the changes in unit cost caused by fluctuating production levels.

In a direct cost system, the product cost remains constant (except when there is a curvilinear cost behavior pattern) for each unit produced, and the

I. Basic data

Semifixed expense budgets for production segments

Department	Weekly Production (units)	Weekly Semifixed Cost Level
A	0–500	1,200
	500–700	1,600
	700–900	2,000
B	0–300	1,400
	300–600	1,700
	600–900	2,000
C	0–400	1,500
	400–700	2,000
	700–900	2,500

Standard product cost

| | Department | | | |
	A	B	C	Total
Material	$2	$ 6	$4	$12
Labor	4	3	2	9
Overhead	1	4	2	7
	$7	$13	$8	$28

Current scheduled production for the coming month

Week 1   650
Week 2   850
Week 3   750
Week 4   550

Details of special offer received

Customer offers to purchase 400 units at a price of $30 per unit.
Units will be produced as follows: week 1, 200 units; week 4, 200 units.

II. Analysis of special offer

Revenue (400 units × $30)	$12,000
Variable cost increase (400 × $28)	11,200
Marginal income	800

Fixed cost increase

	Week 1	Week 4	Total	
Costs for planned production with special offer	$6,500	$6,500	$13,000	
Costs without special offer	5,600	5,300	10,900	
Cost increase	$ 900	$1,200	$ 2,100	2,100
Loss on special offer				($1,300)

Figure 15-3

period costs remain constant for each time period.* The two are never mixed because fixed costs are incurred to support all the activities the firm undertakes to make a profit. No amount of fixed cost is incurred solely for the benefit of one unit of product; thus there is no reason for an accountant to attempt to split off a piece of any fixed cost to attach it to a specific unit of product, especially since fixed costs are divisible only in relation to time and not in relation to production volume.

Consequently, only the variable costs that are directly traceable to a unit of product are included in the unit cost. This product cost includes all variable costs incurred throughout the production plant which are affected by the manufacture of the product. Service department costs as well as production department costs are included. The direct product cost measures the increase in total company manufacturing cost caused by the production of one more unit of product. This cost is similar to the marginal cost used by economists in their analyses. In fact, when curvilinear cost functions are incorporated into the product cost standards, the accountant's standard direct product cost and the economist's marginal cost are identical, because standard product costs are based on expected future events just as marginal costs are. Historical average direct costs are not related to marginal costs because historical costs look to the past instead of to the future.

In addition to the idea that costs are related to units of product, direct cost systems are built on the assumption that costs are direct to people.

* F. C. Lawrence and E. N. Humphreys, *Marginal Costing* London: Macdonald and Evans, 1947), published 25 years ago, includes a most interesting presentation of this idea and of several other direct cost concepts.

People make decisions, and decisions cause costs to be incurred; thus the direct cost system is designed to report to company managers the economic consequences of the decisions they have made. The decisions an individual makes determine the costs he influences, and he is never charged with an expense that his decisions did not influence. Department supervisors are charged with the costs of the labor, material, and overhead that are traceable to their departments, but they are not charged with building depreciation or plant administration, which are not directly influenced by such supervisors' decisions. However, any service department costs that are incurred because of a decision made by a production department supervisor are charged to that production department.

The cost results of the decisions made at the various management levels in the manufacturing plant are periodically summarized in performance reports. These reports tell the factory segment managers the dollar amount of costs that their decisions caused the company to incur during the reporting period. When budget and standards data are included in the reports, the segment managers are able to identify costs that appear to be unreasonable. This helps the manager to isolate the decisions that caused excess costs or that reduced company costs. Managers who have several individuals reporting to them receive a summary of their subordinates' performances.

Much the same system is used in marketing reports. Only costs that are affected by the decisions of a marketing segment manager are charged to his segment, and only the revenue that results from his selling decisions is credited to his segment. The combination of these two factors results in the segment contribution, an amount that measures the contribution of the marketing segment to common costs and profits. Contribution accounting is based on the assumption that the enterprise as a whole can earn a profit, but company segments can only contribute to that profit. Profit represents the result of the total efforts of the manufacturing and marketing functions during a period. Each unit sold and each segment in which units are sold contribute to a pool from which profit finally emerges. Decisions made by managers in the marketing function influence manufacturing cost by causing more or fewer units to be produced. Therefore, marketing segments are charged with the standard costs of the units sold by them; any fluctuations in unit manufacturing costs remain in the production function. If actual production costs are charged to the marketing segments, the contribution generated by a marketing segment will result from a combination of decisions made in production and marketing. Any resulting increases or decreases in marketing contribution will be difficult to trace to the decisions that caused the fluctuation, thereby making the report almost useless.

Costs and revenues are reported to individuals to influence their behavior. The accountant's purpose in preparing a report for a segment manager is to change the behavior of that manager; the accountant does not "just present the facts" with his reports. He is actively seeking to manipulate the behavior of the managers who receive the reports. Direct cost and contribution reports are far more effective than absorption cost reports in affecting management behavior because the direct cost system reports to an individual the costs and revenues that are affected by his decisions. Because he can do something about the costs and revenues that appear in such reports, the manager is likely to be influenced in the manner desired by the accountant who prepared the documents. An absorption cost report, on the other hand, includes all sorts of material that is unaffected by the manager's decisions. It is no wonder that managers either ignore or become confused by absorption cost reports instead of doing what the accountant wants them to do.

Besides reporting cost and revenue data to the decision makers who affected these data with their decisions, the direct cost system provides a data classification scheme that relates costs and revenues to the objects or activities that cause the costs and revenues (e.g., unit costs). Cost–volume–profit analyses, product mix analyses, special offer analyses, and make-or-buy analyses are easy to perform because of the data present in the accounting system. The engineers are not obliged to develop a separate cost system to accumulate data for product mix decisions, nor is there any need for the marketing department to develop a system for keeping track of fixed and variable costs. All the economic data needed for the decisions made in these segments is included in the direct cost system. The data analysis required to develop costs for the various quantitative techniques now being used is easy to perform on the data collected by the direct cost system. In fact, a well-designed direct cost and contribution system provides all the economic data needed for decisions that require historical cost and revenue data. The system does provide a truly integrated management accounting system.

INDEX